MOVIDA
COCINA

SPANISH FLAVOURS FROM FIVE KITCHENS
FRANK CAMORRA AND RICHARD CORNISH

MURDOCH BOOKS

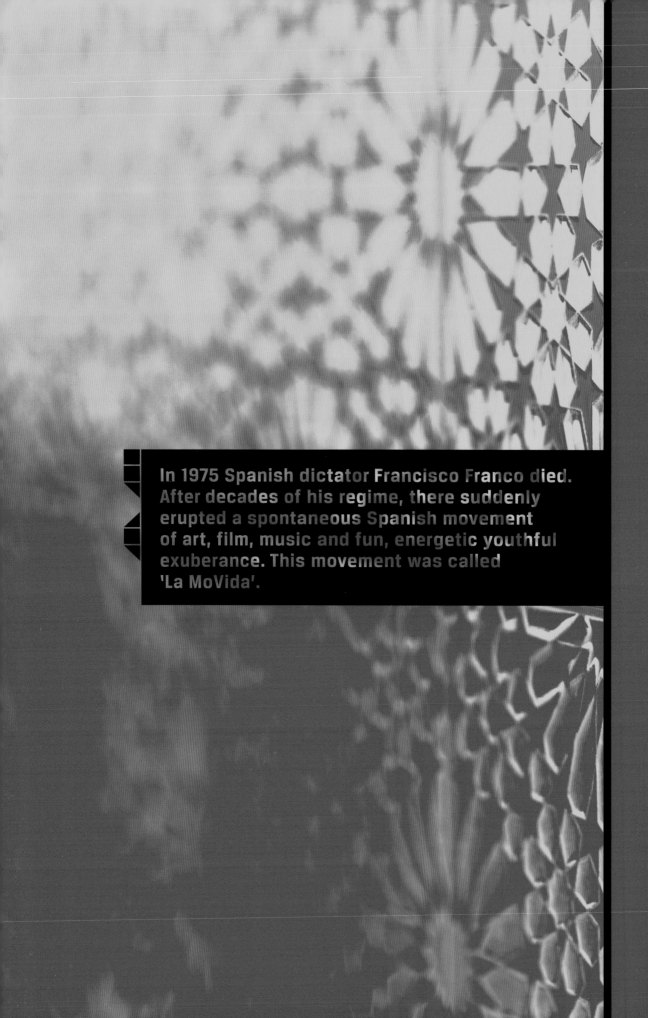

In 1975 Spanish dictator Francisco Franco died. After decades of his regime, there suddenly erupted a spontaneous Spanish movement of art, film, music and fun, energetic youthful exuberance. This movement was called 'La MoVida'.

The sun hits the sandstone dome of the Supreme Court, the cupola balancing on its columns, its top trimmed in ageing terracotta. With the pigeons and plane trees we could be anywhere. It's the slightly comic scene in the street below our kitchen however that anchors us in Melbourne: Dan our charcoal man is in his truck, tapping his fingers on the steering wheel, waiting for the wig-clad barristers and their client, shielding his face from the media circus, to pass by and make way for his delivery. We buy a lot of charcoal from Dan. For at the heart of MoVida Aqui is a charcoal grill and, once lit, she needs feeding from before lunch to last orders. It's an outdated mode of cooking that the Spanish have never given up, but it's part of who we are. Behind the charcoal grill is our great bratt pan, a kind of giant frying pan, in which we slowly make the sofrito for our paella. Next to that is a brand-new sous-vide water bath. Ancient, traditional and modern, side by side in our kitchen, an amalgam of the techniques and ideas.

---- This book is a snapshot of what is happening at MoVida here and now. The shoot, recipe testing and writing for the book took place in just one short month. We wanted to capture the essence of what a restaurant is. A lot of the recipes come from our latest addition, MoVida Aqui, our big restaurant looking out to the Supreme Court, but many also come from the chefs at MoVida Next Door, La Terraza (our freestanding kiosk between Aqui and the Supreme Court), the original MoVida in graffiti-covered Hosier Lane and my family kitchen.

---- Cooking is a creative process and the dishes in this book reflect the way we work together. Sometimes a dish is a collaboration with the team getting together to make the flavours, textures and appearance work in harmony. Sometimes a dish will evolve, changing a little each time it is made to discover its own sense of perfection. Other times, a chef will have a moment of sheer brilliant inspiration. Occasionally we allow ourselves to be influenced by the dishes of chefs we respect. Someone once said to me, "It's only plagiarism if you don't acknowledge it."

---- Although we have several autonomous kitchens, each with a head chef whose dishes reflect their personality, the chefs are united by a single theme. They all know instinctively that they must cook with the seasons. They must not only respect the products but also understand them. They must have an understanding of a sense of place of where the food comes from and the traditions surrounding the food.

---- If there is one thing we are striving for at MoVida, apart from having seriously good fun with food, it is a sense of deliciousness. Everything you eat should be good. There's no room for mediocrity. Everything has to be delicious.

Mum and Dad are from the south of Spain but were working in Barcelona when I was born. They headed back down to Andalusia when I was still a babe and then moved to Australia when I was four. Mum has kept a Spanish kitchen ever since they moved here. It is based on traditional Spanish frugal extravagance. This means lots and lots of wonderful tasting delicious food made from the simplest ingredients. Breakfast would be orange juice, coffee and perhaps toast with olive oil or manteca, the spicy fat saved from cooking chorizo. But that wasn't our first breakfast for the day. Spaniards have more than one breakfast; one at home, one a little bit later and another perhaps to segue into the next meal. It's never a lot of dishes eaten at once; just a lot of small bites spread across the morning. Like all Spanish food, there are no hard and fast rules because breakfast for some could be as simple as a cigarette and a glass of brandy. This is the type of organised chaos we revere. We serve the breakfast dishes in this chapter at our little outdoor kiosk, La Terraza.

DESAYUNO
BREAKFAST

ORANGE JUICE

SERVES 4

ZUMO DE NARANJA

3 KG (6 LB 12 OZ/ABOUT 12) ORANGES

This is the first smell of the Spanish morning. Vibrant and alive. Sweet and sharp. Without ice it's unadulterated to the last drop. A perfect zumo de naranja is so good it makes you question why you'd juice any other fruit.

Chill the oranges in the refrigerator overnight. This way you won't need ice in your glass.

The next day, cut each orange in half and juice by hand or with a mechanical juicer. Remove the seeds from the pulp and discard. Add the pulp back to the juice and stir. Pour into glasses. Smell.

12

BRIOCHE

55 ML (1¾ FL OZ) MILK

28 G (1 OZ) FRESH YEAST (SEE GLOSSARY)

5 EGGS

225 G (8 OZ/1½ CUPS) PLAIN (ALL-PURPOSE) FLOUR, PLUS EXTRA FOR DUSTING

225 G (8 OZ/1½ CUPS) BAKER'S FLOUR (SEE GLOSSARY)

58 G (2 OZ) CASTER (SUPERFINE) SUGAR

10 G (⅓ OZ) COOKING SALT

143 G (5½ OZ) UNSALTED BUTTER, CUT INTO 2 CM (¾ INCH) CUBES AND SOFTENED

BUTTER AND JAM, TO SERVE

The Spanish love to dunk. Put a café con leche and a pastry in front of them and the pastry will always end up in the coffee. This is an easy brioche recipe and tastes like the brioche served in the cafés in Madrid.

Heat the milk in a saucepan over medium heat until lukewarm. Pour into a small bowl and crumble in the yeast. Mash together with a fork until the yeast has dissolved. Set aside for 15 minutes or until the mixture is foamy. Lightly beat 4 eggs and set aside.

Attach a dough hook to an electric mixer. Sift the flours, sugar and salt into the bowl of the mixer and mix on low speed for 2 minutes to further aerate. With the motor running, gradually add the yeast mixture and beaten egg to the bowl. Continue mixing on low speed for another 6 minutes. With the motor running, add the butter, a cube at a time, then increase the speed to medium and continue mixing for 9 minutes. The dough should be smooth and shiny. Form into a tight ball, cover the bowl with a clean tea (dish) towel. Set aside to prove in a warm place for 1 hour or until doubled in size.

Place the dough on a lightly floured bench and knock down the dough by gently kneading it for 30 seconds. Form into a tight ball and return to the bowl. Cover again and allow to prove for another hour or until the dough increases to 1½ times its size.

Line a 28 cm x 9 cm (11¼ inch x 3½ inch) bread tin with baking paper. Divide the dough into 3 equal portions and roll into tight balls. Place the balls, side by side, in the bread tin, cover and set aside to prove in a warm space for another 1½ hours.

Preheat the oven to 180°C (350°F/Gas 4).

Lightly beat the remaining egg with a pinch of salt to make an eggwash. Brush the top of the dough with the eggwash and bake for 25 minutes or until cooked through. To test if it's ready, remove the loaf from the tin while it's still hot and tap the base with your knuckles; it should sound hollow. Cool on a wire rack for 45 minutes.

To serve, cut into thick slices and toast each side under a hot grill (broiler) for 1 minute or until golden. (Brioche tends to burn in a toaster.) Serve with butter and lashings of jam or Seville orange marmalade.

TOAST WITH MAJORCAN SAUSAGE

330 G (11¾ OZ) FRESH CHORIZO	2 BAY LEAVES
(SEE GLOSSARY)	200 G (7 OZ) PIMIENTOS DE PIQUILLO
200 G (7 OZ) TOCINO (PORK BACK FAT)	(SEE GLOSSARY), DRAINED
(SEE GLOSSARY)	1 TABLESPOON SHERRY VINEGAR
3 GARLIC CLOVES	1 TEASPOON SEA SALT FLAKES
2 TABLESPOONS SMOKED SWEET PAPRIKA	1 TABLESPOON FINELY GROUND BLACK PEPPER
(PIMENTÓN, SEE GLOSSARY)	TOASTED BOCADILLOS, TO SERVE (SEE PAGE 38)

MAKES ABOUT 2 CUPS

TOSTADAS CON SOBRASADA

Sobrasada is a fermented pork sausage from Majorca. Rich, raw and spicy, it's delicious spread over toast. We couldn't put a recipe for a raw fermented sausage in this book so, after a bit of experimentation, we came up with a version that almost perfectly replicates the porky goodness of the real sobrasada.

Remove the casing from the chorizo and discard. Roughly chop the filling. Chop the tocino into 1 cm (½ inch) cubes and place in a high-density plastic bag with the chorizo, 2 garlic cloves, paprika and bay leaves. Follow our steps on sous-vide cooking (see page 123). Vacuum seal the bag and cook in a water bath at 80°C (176°F) for 10 hours.

Remove the bag from the water bath and allow to cool slightly. Transfer the contents of the bag, discardind the bay leaves, into a food processor. Finely chop the remaining garlic clove and add to the food processor with the pimientos, vinegar, salt and pepper and process on high speed for 10 minutes or until a smooth paste forms. Check for seasoning, then transfer to a bowl. Spoon the mixture onto the toasted bocadillos to serve.

The sobrasada will keep for up to 4 days in an airtight container in the fridge or freeze for up to 2 months.

SARDINES ON TOAST

SERVES 4

TOSTADOS DA SARDINILLAS

4 RIPE TOMATOES, PEELED AND SEEDED (SEE GLOSSARY)	2 X 120 G (4¼ OZ) CANS SARDINILLAS (SEE GLOSSARY), DRAINED
SEA SALT FLAKES	8 PIMIENTOS DE PIQUILLO (SEE GLOSSARY), TORN INTO THIRDS
EXTRA VIRGIN OLIVE OIL, FOR DRIZZLING	
½ BAGUETTE (SEE PAGES 38–9)	2 GARLIC CLOVES, SKIN ON, HALVED

Spanish canned sardines are so good you eat them bones and all. Toast some bread, rub it with garlic (leave the garlic skin on so your fingers don't end up smelling of garlic), spoon over some fresh tomato purée and top with a few sharp peppers and some fat little Spanish sardines. Now you're right to face the day.

Using a vegetable grater placed over a large bowl, grate the tomatoes like a carrot. Season with salt, drizzle with olive oil and stir to combine. Set aside.

Preheat a grill (broiler) to high. Cut the pointy end off the baguette and discard or use for crumbs. Cut the baguette into 2 even pieces, then halve each lengthways. Place the baguettes, cut-side up, under the grill and toast until golden.

Place the sardines and pimientos on a small baking tray lined with baking paper and grill for 1 minute or until warm. Season with salt.

Rub the cut side of the garlic onto the toasted side of the baguettes and drizzle each with oil. Spoon some tomato purée onto each baguette, then top with about 5 sardines and 6 pieces of pimiento. Sprinkle with salt and drizzle with a little more oil and serve straight away.

MICHAEL
PASTRY

Like most pastry chefs, Michael arrives at work when it's still dark. The only time I have been in the kitchen early enough to see Chef Michael start work was when the Spanish football team played against the Dutch in the 2010 FIFA World Cup and the kick-off was 4 am local time.

----- As soon as Chef Michael arrives, he turns on the kitchen lights and ovens and gets baking. From his few square metres of bench space in La Terraza kitchen, he produces all the bread, baguettes, bocadillos, brioche, croissants and desserts for both the kiosk and MoVida Aqui. He is perfectly at home in the heat and steam of the ovens, among the rattle and hum of the provers and mixers. His work is measured, methodical and mathematical. He balances the hard toil of kneading and shaping loaves with the delicate precision of making pastries. His work is like ballet in which learned, rehearsed and well-practised moves are performed: kneading, rolling, lifting and layering.

----- He's calm and still like a mill pond with a subtle dry sense of English humour; all desirable traits honed while working in London kitchens where chefs swear and throw knives and saucepans. He's seen that inferno of screaming chefs and flying fry pans. His life is different now.

----- He watches the weather like a hawk because he knows a low-pressure system coming in from the west will affect how his bread rises.

----- He treats his sourdough mother like a member of staff, greeting it and feeding it every morning. He has done the hard yards, has earned his stripes and has nothing to prove but his dough.

MAJORCAN PASTRIES

MAKES 10 ENSAIMADAS

125 ML (4 FL OZ/½ CUP) MILK	5 G (⅛ OZ) SALT
25 G (1 OZ) FRESH YEAST (SEE GLOSSARY)	PLAIN (ALL-PURPOSE) FLOUR, FOR DUSTING
2 EGGS	60 G (2¼ OZ) DUCK FAT, AT ROOM TEMPERATURE
2 TEASPOONS EXTRA VIRGIN OLIVE OIL	JAM, TO SERVE
315 G (11 OZ) BAKER'S FLOUR (SEE GLOSSARY)	150 G (5⅓ OZ) ICING (CONFECTIONER'S) SUGAR
38 G (1¼ OZ) CASTER (SUPERFINE) SUGAR	

We have wanted to serve this light Majorcan escargot for years but needed a kitchen big enough to hire a pastry chef. Finally with the opening of Aqui and La Terraza, it was possible. Chef Michael kneads, rolls and folds lard or duck fat into the pastry, then rolls it into a snail shape. Slightly sweet and golden, these are best eaten while still a little warm.

Heat the milk in a saucepan over medium heat until lukewarm. Pour the milk into a small bowl and crumble in the yeast. Mash together with a fork until the yeast has dissolved completely. Set aside for 15 minutes or until the mixture is foamy.

Beat 1 egg and add to the yeast mixture with the oil and mix well.

Attach a dough hook to an electric mixer. Sift the flour, sugar and salt into the bowl of the mixer and mix on low speed for 1 minute to further aerate. With the motor running, add the yeast mixture. Continue mixing on low speed for 4 minutes, then increase the speed to medium and mix for another 4 minutes or until the dough is elastic. Form into a tight ball, cover the bowl with a clean tea (dish) towel. Set aside to prove in a warm place for 1 hour or until doubled in size.

Lightly flour a cold bench. Using a rolling pin, roll the dough out to make a 3 mm (⅛ inch) thick (or as thin as you can get it without tearing), 50 cm x 30 cm (20 inch x 12 inch) rectangle. Using a plastic dough scraper, spread the duck fat evenly over the dough as if spreading butter over toast, spreading right to the very edges. Place the rectangle with a long edge closest to you. Starting at the long edge furthest away from you, gently fold the dough over by about 1 cm (½ inch) towards you. Place your fingers loosely curled behind the rolled edge to support it, then use your thumbs to pinch the seam together as you push the dough back away from you very slightly, tightening it into a tidy roll. Continue rolling the dough towards you and pushing back at the seam to tighten after each roll. Try to keep the dough edges as neat as possible to maintain a rectangular shape; use your fingers to smooth out any edges that poke out as you're rolling. The dough should now resemble a thin uncooked baguette.

Now pick up the dough baguette at each end and gently pull it until it is about 90 cm (35½ inches) long and 3 cm (1¼ inches) in diameter. Place back on the bench and cut in half to create 2 x 45 cm (17¾ inch) long rolls. Place on a tray, cover with a clean tea towel and refrigerate for 20 minutes to firm up the fat.

Lightly flour the bench again. Cut each roll into 5 x 9 cm (3½ inch) long portions. With flat palms, roll each portion, using a quick back and forth motion, to form a thin snake, about 40 cm (16 inches) long. Starting at one end, coil the dough into a snail-like shape and tuck the tail under. Carefully lift 5 ensaimadas and place onto a baking tray lined with baking paper, allowing plenty of room for spreading. Repeat with the remaining ensaimadas. Cover the trays with a clean tea towel and set aside to prove in a warm place for 1½ hours or until the dough increases by 1½ times its size.

Preheat the oven to 160°C (315°F/Gas 2–3). Lightly beat the remaining egg with a pinch of salt to make an eggwash. Lightly brush the tops of the ensaimadas with the eggwash and bake for 12 minutes or until they have a good crust. To test if they're ready, tap the bases with your knuckles; they should sound hollow. Cool a little on wire racks. Dust them with the icing sugar and serve warm with your favourite jam. Enjoy with a cup of hot carajillo (sweet milk coffee with a dash of brandy).

CHURROS WITH HOT CHOCOLATE

CHURROS

250 ML (9 FL OZ/1 CUP) MILK

80 G (2¾ OZ) BUTTER

110 G (3¾ OZ/½ CUP) CASTER (SUPERFINE) SUGAR

COOKING SALT

1 VANILLA BEAN

150 G (5½ OZ/1 CUP) PLAIN (ALL-PURPOSE) FLOUR, SIFTED

3 EGGS, LIGHTLY BEATEN

½ TEASPOON GROUND CINNAMON

SUNFLOWER OR OTHER MILD-FLAVOURED OIL, FOR DEEP-FRYING

HOT CHOCOLATE

1 LITRE (35 FL OZ/4 CUPS) MILK

200 G (7 OZ) SPANISH DRINKING CHOCOLATE (SEE GLOSSARY), BROKEN INTO SMALL PIECES

SERVES 6-8

CHURROS CON CHOCOLATE

I don't know how many times my Spanish customers have told me that churros are not dessert. "They are for breakfast!" they say. "I can't remember how many times I have been in Spain and eaten churros late, late at night!" I reply. Eat them whenever.

To make the churros, heat the milk and butter in a saucepan over medium heat until the butter is melted. Add 10 g (⅓ oz) of the sugar and a pinch of salt. Cut the vanilla bean in half and scrape out the seeds with the tip of a sharp knife, then add both the bean and seeds to the pan and bring to the boil. Straight away remove from the heat, remove the vanilla bean and discard. Add the flour and whisk together, whisking hard to make sure no lumps form.

Return the pan to low heat and beat continuously with a wooden spoon for 5 minutes or until the dough comes away from the side of the pan. Remove from the heat and allow to cool for 2 minutes. Add the beaten egg, a little at a time, incorporating well after each addition before adding more. Set aside.

Combine the remaining sugar and cinnamon in a small shallow bowl. Set aside.

To make the hot chocolate, warm the milk in a saucepan over low heat. Add the chocolate and stir until just melted. Simmer, whisking occasionally, for 20–25 minutes or until thickened. Reduce the heat to very low and set the saucepan just off the heat to keep warm.

Meanwhile, fill a large heavy-based saucepan or deep-fryer one-third full with oil and heat to 170°C (325°F), or until a cube of bread dropped into the oil takes 20 seconds to turn golden.

Spoon the dough into a piping bag fitted with a 1 cm (½ inch) broad star nozzle, making sure there are no air pockets in the bag. Pipe the dough, in batches, into the hot oil, using kitchen scissors to snip the dough off into 15 cm (6 inch) lengths. Deep-fry the churros for 1–2 minutes each side or until golden all over. Drain on paper towel and sprinkle liberally with the cinnamon sugar.

To serve, whisk the hot chocolate, pour into cups and dunk the hot churros in.

SPINACH TORTILLA

SERVES 1

TORTILLA DE ESPINACAS

150 G (5½ OZ) BABY SPINACH LEAVES

SEA SALT FLAKES

3 EGGS

1¼ TABLESPOONS EXTRA VIRGIN OLIVE OIL

1 GARLIC CLOVE, FINELY CHOPPED

Every morning, Chef Marty at La Terraza takes delivery of a box of organic eggs laid by hens who free-range on a dairy farm. With them he makes tortillas for breakfast. He watches the eggs like a hawk. He waits for that moment when they are between being runny and just completely set before taking them off the heat.

Wash the spinach several times to remove any grit. Drain and pat dry. Bring a saucepan of lightly salted water to the boil. Blanch the spinach for 30 seconds, then drain and refresh under cold running water. Drain well. Place the spinach in a clean tea (dish) towel and wring out the excess water. Roll the spinach into a ball, place on a chopping board and thinly slice.

Using a fork, lightly beat the eggs with a pinch of salt in a bowl. Set aside.

Heat the oil in a 20 cm (8 inch) non-stick frying pan over low heat. Cook the garlic for 5 minutes or until softened but not browned. Increase the heat to high and add the spinach. Cook for 1 minute, stirring constantly.

Pour the beaten egg into the pan and for the next minute or so, using a flat plastic spatula, fold it through the spinach mixture, bringing the outside of the mixture into the middle of the pan. Reduce the heat to low and cook, without stirring, for 1–2 minutes. Take it off the heat, cover with a lid or plate and leave for 5 minutes to allow the residual heat in the pan to finish cooking the tortilla.

Gently slide the tortilla off the pan onto a warmed plate. Sprinkle with a little salt and serve warm.

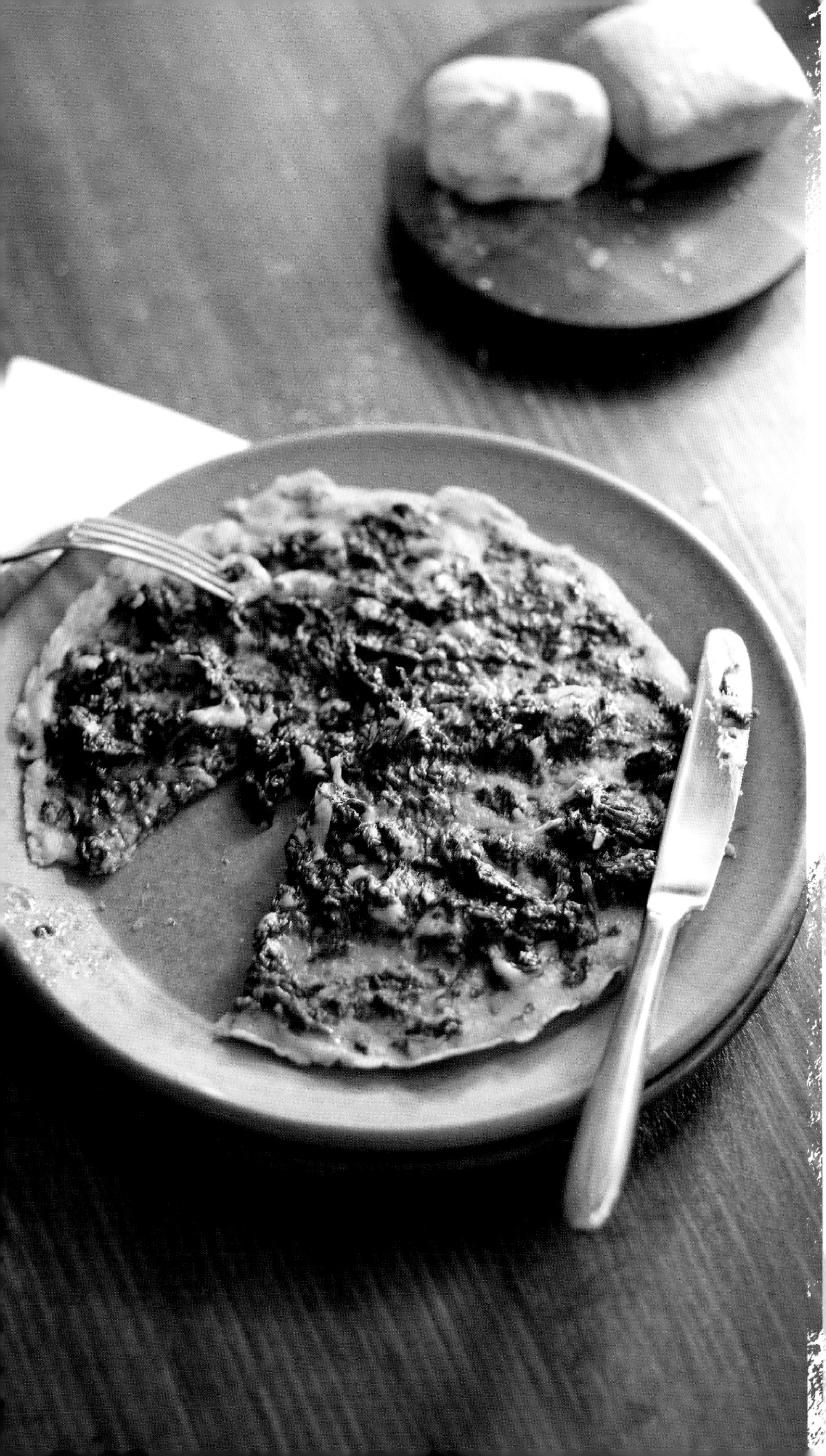

CHORIZO SWIRLS

CARACOLES DE CHORIZO

ROUGH PUFF PASTRY

500 G (1 LB 2 OZ/3⅓ CUPS) PLAIN
  (ALL-PURPOSE) FLOUR, PLUS EXTRA,
  FOR DUSTING
1 TEASPOON SEA SALT
1 TABLESPOON SHERRY VINEGAR
50 G (1¾ OZ) UNSALTED BUTTER,
  AT ROOM TEMPERATURE
350 G (12 OZ) COLD UNSALTED BUTTER, EXTRA

CHORIZO FILLING

1½ TABLESPOONS EXTRA VIRGIN OLIVE OIL
1 BROWN ONION, FINELY DICED
1 GARLIC CLOVE, FINELY CHOPPED
2 X 150 G (5½ OZ) FRESH CHORIZO,
  CUT INTO INTO 5 MM (¼ INCH) CUBES
1 RED CAPSICUM (PEPPER), FINELY DICED
1 GREEN CAPSICUM (PEPPER), FINELY DICED
2 BAY LEAVES
SEA SALT
150 G (5½ OZ) QUESO DE MAHÓN, FINELY GRATED

"Michael, our pastry chef, was making beautiful sweet sultana-filled escargots one morning," says Chef Marty, "and I thought they'd be great with a savoury filling. Everyone loves chorizo so we cooked some in a capsicum sofrito, laid it out over some rough puff pastry and rolled it up and cut out the escargot. Fresh from the oven they go wonderfully with orange juice or a strong coffee, or enjoy later in the day, reheated, with a cold beer."

You will need to begin this recipe the day before.

To make the rough puff pastry, sift the flour and salt into a bowl. Add the vinegar, room temperature butter and 220 ml (7⅓ fl oz) of water and combine very slowly using your hands until a smooth, elastic dough forms. Tip the dough out onto a lightly floured bench and shape the dough into a ball. Place in a clean bowl, cover with plastic wrap and refrigerate for 2 hours.

Meanwhile, make the chorizo filling. Heat the olive oil in a heavy-based pan over medium–low heat. Add the onion and cook, stirring occasionally, for 5–8 minutes or until softened. Add the garlic and chorizo and cook, stirring occasionally, for 8 minutes or until the meat is cooked. Add the capsicum and bay leaves and cook for 15 minutes or until softened. Season with salt, cover and allow to cool, then refrigerate until chilled.

Place the pastry on a cold, well-floured bench and roll it out into a 30 cm (12 inch) square. Shape the extra cold butter into a 15 cm (6 inch) square and place in the centre of the dough. Make a cut from each corner of the butter and spread to each corner of the dough. Fold the outside edges of the pastry over the butter, the two opposite edges first then the other opposite edges, to completely encase it. Using a rolling pin, gently but firmly beat the pastry and butter to form a 15 cm x 45 cm (6 inch x 18 inch) rectangle, making sure the butter remains in between the layers of dough. Measure the pastry into thirds lengthways, then fold the pastry edge closest to you to the top third mark. Now fold the remaining top third over this. Place the dough onto a floured chopping board, cover with plastic wrap and refrigerate for 25 minutes.

Place the pastry on a cold, well-floured bench with the open end facing you and roll the pastry into another 15 cm x 45 cm (6 inch x 18 inch) rectangle, so that the longer edges run away from you. Place back on the floured board, cover and refrigerate for another 25 minutes.

Repeat the chilling, beating into a rectangle, three more times, refrigerating for 25 minutes between each.

To assemble the escargots, first line 2 baking trays with baking paper. Place the pastry on a cold, well-floured bench and roll into a 3 mm (⅛ inch) thick, 30 cm (12 inch) square. Using the back of a spoon, spread the chorizo filling over the pastry to evenly coat the surface and pushing the mixture right to the edges. Sprinkle over the cheese. Starting at the bottom edge, roll the pastry evenly and tightly to form a log with as many layers as possible. Using a very sharp knife, cut the log into 10 x 3 cm (1¼ inch) slices. Place on the lined trays, spacing them at least 7 cm (2¾ inches) apart for them to expand. Cover with plastic wrap and refrigerate for 20 minutes.

Meanwhile, preheat the oven to 170°C (325°F/Gas 3). Bake the escargot for 10 minutes or until the bases are crisp. Remove from the oven and cool on a wire rack.

A bocadillo looks like a bread roll, but it is not. It holds a special place in the Spanish imagination. For a moment, let's compare it to the ideal Anglo sandwich – slices of soft white bread, scantily spread with butter, layered with thin slices of cucumber and served with tea on the lawn. Perhaps there's someone gently punting down the river in the distance.

---- Now take a second to picture the perfect bocadillo. It's a crunchy roll filled with fried calamari and alioli (garlicky mayonnaise), eaten in a raucous bar filled with Real Madrid football supporters and their girlfriends, washed down with a few ice-cold beers at 2 am. A bocadillo could just as easily be a fresh roll filled with potato tortilla, a wedge of Manchego cheese or a few slices of jamón served at a railway station as you wait for your train. Bocadillos are deliciously good Spanish fast food.

BOCADILLOS

ROLLS & SANDWICHES

BASIC BREAD DOUGH

MAKES 20 BOCADILLOS OR 2 BAGUETTES

LA MASA

60 ML (2 FL OZ/¼ CUP) MILK
60 ML (2 FL OZ/¼ CUP) EXTRA VIRGIN OLIVE OIL
20 G (¾ OZ) FRESH YEAST (SEE GLOSSARY)
500 G (1 LB 2 OZ/3⅓ CUPS) BAKER'S FLOUR (SEE GLOSSARY), PLUS EXTRA FOR DUSTING
75 G (2⅝ OZ) FINE SEMOLINA
15 G (½ OZ) COOKING SALT

Good bread starts with good dough. This is a reliable recipe, made in an electric mixer. It produces rolls or baguettes with a firm, golden crust and a moist crumb.

Heat the milk and 300 ml (10½ fl oz) of water in a saucepan over medium heat until lukewarm. Pour into a bowl and add the oil. Crumble in the yeast and mash together with a fork until the yeast has dissolved completely. Set aside for 15 minutes or until the mixture is foamy.

Attach a dough hook to an electric mixer. Sift the flour, semolina and salt into the bowl of the mixer. Mix on low speed to combine, then gradually add the yeast mixture. Continue mixing for 4 minutes, then increase the speed to medium and mix for another 4 minutes. The dough should be quite sticky but elastic. Form into a tight ball, cover the bowl with a clean tea (dish) towel and set aside to prove in a warm place for 1 hour or until doubled in size.

To make bocadillos, knock down the dough to expel excess air. Lightly flour a bench and roll out the dough to a 2.5 cm (1 inch) thick, 25 cm x 20 cm (10 inch x 8 inch) rectangle. Using a dough cutter or sharp knife, cut out 20 x 5 cm (2 inch) squares. Place on lightly floured baking trays, cover with a tea towel and set aside to prove in a warm place for 20 minutes or until doubled in size.

Preheat the oven to 190°C (375°F/Gas 5). Lightly dust the rolls with flour and bake for 15 minutes or until lightly golden. Cool on wire racks.

To make baguettes, divide the dough into 2 equal pieces and knock down each piece to expel excess air. Lightly flour a bench and use your hands to flatten each piece to make a 2.5 cm (1 inch) thick, 33 cm x 13 cm (13 inch x 5 inch) rectangle. Cover each with a tea towel and allow to rest for 10 minutes.

Working with one rectangle at a time, place a long edge closest to you. Imagine 3 horizontal lines dividing the rectangle into quarters. To form the baguette, start at the long edge of the dough furthest away from you. If you are right-handed, using your left hand, and working right to left, start to fold the long edge towards the first imaginary line, straight away follow with the heel of your right hand, stamping downwards to seal the fold. Continue this motion until you reach the left-hand side and the whole edge has been rolled over and sealed into a neat cylinder. If you are left-handed, start on the left-hand side, rolling with your right and stamping with your left.

Repeat the rolling and stamping twice more. When you have reached the edge of the dough closest to you, stamp down along the edges to seal the baguette, which should now be about 40 cm (16 inches) long. Pinch together any gaps at the pointy ends of the baguette. Repeat with the other rectangle of dough. Place the baguettes, seam-side down, on a lightly floured baking tray, cover with a tea towel and allow to prove in a warm place for 30 minutes or until doubled in size.

Preheat the oven to 190°C (375°F/Gas 5). Lightly dust the baguettes with flour and bake for 25 minutes or until golden and the bases sound hollow when tapped. Cool on a wire rack.

TOASTED HAM & CHEESE SANDWICHES WITH TRUFFLE

200 G (7 OZ) BUFFALO MOZZARELLA

BUTTER, SOFTENED, FOR SPREADING

8 SLICES WHITE BREAD

8 SLICES JAMÓN SERRANO

4 G FRESH BLACK TRUFFLE, FINELY GRATED

SEA SALT FLAKES

SERVES 4

BIKINI

These are a Barcelonan specialty. They're called bikinis because they are teeny weeny triangles of toasted sandwich. The best bikinis I've ever sampled are at Carles Abellan's Tapaç 24 in Barcelona: buffalo mozzarella, good-quality jamón and the merest hint of freshly grated truffle. This is our homage to their spectacular little sandwich.

Preheat a sandwich press to medium–high.

Slice the mozzarella into 12 slices. Butter both sides of each slice of bread and lay out on a bench. Top half the slices each with 2 slices of jamón and 3 slices of mozzarella and scatter over about one-quarter of the truffle. Season with salt and sandwich with the remaining slices.

Toast in the sandwich press for 4–5 minutes or until golden and the mozzarella is melted. Trim the crusts off and discard. Cut into 4 triangles and serve hot. Excellent with a glass of cava.

ROASTED CAPSICUM & SOFT-BOILED EGG ROLLS

SERVES 4-6

BOCADILLOS DE PIMIENTOS ASADOS Y HUEVOS COCIDOS

2 RED CAPSICUM (PEPPERS)	2½ TABLESPOONS CHARDONNAY VINEGAR
2 GREEN CAPSICUM (PEPPERS)	4 RIPE TOMATOES, PEELED, SEEDED
1 BROWN ONION, UNPEELED	(SEE GLOSSARY) AND ROUGHLY DICED
125 ML (4 FL OZ/½ CUP) EXTRA VIRGIN	⅓ CUP OREGANO LEAVES
OLIVE OIL	2 GARLIC CLOVES
SEA SALT FLAKES	6 EGGS
½ TABLESPOON FENNEL SEEDS	2 BAGUETTES (SEE PAGES 38-9)

This is a sandwich Mum used to make for me when I lived at home: a crusty roll filled with rich moist roasted vegetables. If you have time, make the roasted capsicum filling the night before for the flavours to develop – it tastes even better after a few days.

Preheat the oven to 185°C (365°F/Gas 4–5). Place the capsicum and onion in a roasting tray, drizzle with 2 tablespoons of the olive oil and sprinkle with salt. Roast for 30 minutes or until the capsicum are slightly charred. Remove the capsicum, place in a bowl and cover with plastic wrap to lightly steam; this will make them easier to peel. Continue roasting the onion for 15 minutes or until very soft. Remove, add to the capsicum and tip in any juices from the tray.

Spread the fennel seeds on a baking tray and roast in the oven for 5 minutes or until aromatic. Roughly chop.

When the capsicum and onion are cool enough to handle, peel away the skins from the capsicum and discard with the stalks and seeds. Remove and discard the outer skin of the onion. Cut the capsicum and onion flesh into 2.5 cm (1 inch) thick strips. Return the vegetables to the bowl with any juices and gently mix together with the remaining oil, vinegar, tomato, fennel seeds and a good pinch of salt. Roughly chop the oregano and garlic and combine with the vegetables. (At this stage, the mixture can be covered with plastic wrap and refrigerated overnight.)

Place the eggs in a large saucepan of cold water over high heat. Bring to the boil and cook for 3 minutes. Remove and refresh in cold water. When cool enough to handle, peel, quarter and add to the vegetables.

Trim the ends off the baguettes. Cut the baguette into two 15 cm (6 inch) pieces (to serve 4) or three 10 cm (4 inch) pieces (to serve 6). Halve each piece lengthways.

To serve, divide the filling between the baguette bases, spoon over a little dressing from the bowl, sprinkle with salt and sandwich with the tops.

ROASTED VEGETABLE & ANCHOVY ROLLS

1 RED CAPSICUM (PEPPER)	2 ZUCCHINI (COURGETTES), CUT INTO 3 CM (1¼ INCH) LENGTHS
1 BROWN ONION, UNPEELED	
60 ML (2 FL OZ/¼ CUP) EXTRA VIRGIN OLIVE OIL	3 LEBANESE EGGPLANT (AUBERGINES), CUT INTO 3 CM (1¼ INCH) LENGTHS
SEA SALT FLAKES	1 RIPE WHOLE TOMATO
1 LARGE FENNEL BULB, CUT INTO 2.5 CM (1 INCH) WEDGES	6 ANCHOVY FILLETS, PLUS 4-6 FOR GARNISHING
1 GARLIC BULB	⅓ CUP OREGANO LEAVES
	2 BAGUETTES (SEE PAGES 38-9)

MAKES 4-6

BOCADILLOS DE VERDURAS CON ANCHOAS

This is a little meal in itself — showing the rustic hearty origin of the bocadillo — a farm worker's lunch. Sweet, rich, roasted and moist vegetables are tempered with the salty hit of a little anchovy. The bread soaks up the juices giving you a meaty, heavy filling surrounded by a golden crust.

Preheat the oven to 185°C (365°F/Gas 4-5). Place the capsicum and onion in a roasting tray, drizzle with the oil and sprinkle with salt. Roast for 30 minutes or until the capsicum is slightly charred. Remove the capsicum, place in a bowl and cover with plastic wrap to lightly steam; this will make it easier to peel.

Add the fennel and garlic bulb to the onion and continue roasting for 15 minutes. Add the zucchini, eggplant, tomato and 3 anchovies and mix together to coat the vegetables with the oil and cooking juices. Roast for 35–40 minutes or until the vegetables are soft and aromatic. Set aside.

When the vegetables are cool enough to handle, remove and discard the outer skin of the onion. Cut the onion into 2 cm (¾ inch) thick strips and return to the tray. Peel the tomato and discard the skin. Crush the flesh with a fork and return to the tray. Squeeze the garlic cloves from their skins into the tray. Peel away the skin from the capsicum and discard with the stalks and seeds. Tear the flesh into 3 cm (1¼ inch) thick strips and add to the tray. Roughly chop the remaining anchovies and add to the tray with the oregano. Stir to combine well and check the seasoning.

Trim the ends off the baguettes. Cut each baguette into two 15 cm (6 inch) pieces (to serve 4) or three 10 cm (4 inch) pieces (to serve 6). Halve each piece lengthways.

To serve, divide the filling between the bases, spoon over a little of the liquid from the vegetables, arrange an extra anchovy on top and sandwich with the tops.

MARINATED CHICKEN SANDWICHES

MAKES 6

BOCADILLOS DE POLLO EN ESCABECHE

2 RED ONIONS	**SEA SALT FLAKES**
60 ML (2 FL OZ/¼ CUP) EXTRA VIRGIN OLIVE OIL	**2 X 250 G (9 OZ) SKINLESS CHICKEN**
4 BAY LEAVES	**BREAST FILLETS**
2 GARLIC CLOVES, THINLY SLICED	**270 G (9½ OZ/1 CUP) ALIOLI (SEE PAGE 54)**
SMALL PINCH OF SAFFRON THREADS	**¼ CUP PARSLEY LEAVES, CHOPPED**
1 LARGE CARROT, CUT INTO 5 CM (2 INCH)	**TABASCO SAUCE, TO TASTE**
LENGTHS AND CUT INTO JULIENNE	**12 SLICES SOURDOUGH BREAD**
250 ML (9 FL OZ/1 CUP) WHITE WINE VINEGAR	**GUINDILLAS (SEE GLOSSARY), DRAINED,**
250 ML (9 FL OZ/1 CUP) DRY WHITE WINE	**TO SERVE**
1 TABLESPOON BLACK PEPPERCORNS	

Years ago, long before fridges were invented, people would preserve food in vinegar. Escabeche echoes this technique, although these days it's more about flavouring than preserving. Chef Marty at La Terraza takes slices of crusty bread and fills them with this rich mix of sharp poached chicken and vegetables combined with garlicky alioli.

You will need to begin this recipe the day before.

Cut the onions into 5 mm (¼ inch) thick wedges. Heat the oil in a heavy-based frying pan over medium–low heat. Add the onion, bay leaves, garlic and saffron. Cover and cook, stirring occasionally, for 15 minutes or until the onion is soft and translucent. Do not allow the onion to brown. Add the carrot, cover and cook for 15 minutes or until the carrot begins to soften. Add the vinegar, wine, peppercorns, 250 ml (9 fl oz/1 cup) of water and 1 teaspoon salt. Increase the heat to high and bring to the boil. Reduce the heat and simmer for 15 minutes to concentrate the flavours and cook out the vinegar and wine. Add the chicken and cook for 20–25 minutes or until cooked through. Remove from the heat and allow to cool slightly. Transfer to a non-reactive bowl, cover with plastic wrap and refrigerate overnight.

The next day, tip the mixture into a sieve placed over a bowl, reserving both the solids and liquid. Remove and discard the bay leaves and peppercorns. Shred the chicken into 5 cm x 5 mm (2 inch x ¼ inch) strips and place in a bowl. Add the onion and carrot to the chicken, along with the alioli, parsley and 100 ml (3½ fl oz) of the reserved cooking liquid. Mix well and check for seasoning.

To serve, divide the mixture between half of the slices of sourdough. Sprinkle each with a few drops of Tabasco and sandwich with the remaining slices of sourdough. Cut each sandwich in half and serve with the guindillas.

La Terraza is like a classic family-run Spanish bar in the heart of Melbourne's CBD. It's our freestanding kiosk on a square dominated by a bank tower and the dome of the Supreme Court. What it lacks in terracotta tiles and bullfighting posters it makes up for in its natural daily rhythm that follows the changing pace of the day. Inside the kitchen is Chef Marty, a close mate who I have known since our apprentice days. He shows his skills by turning out different styles of food on the head of a pin. At breakfast he's working side by side with Chef Michael, our pastry chef, cooking silky smooth huevos revueltos (scrambled eggs) and little tostadas. Deliveries come in from the veg man and within a few short hours he has half a dozen different beautiful seasonal salads lined up for lunch along with a repertoire of slow-cooked dishes. It's an open kitchen, so customers sit at the bar and talk to Marty and Emma, who runs the front-of-house. She's a gem. She came across from MoVida at Hosier Lane and makes this little part of Melbourne sing.

---- Behind the coffee machine is Chad. With his blonde locks and puppy face covered in all manifestations of facial hair he reminds me of the luckdragon from *The NeverEnding Story*.

---- They work like a family. On a Friday night when the sun makes its way over the Supreme Court and the offices start to empty, Marty retreats to the hot end of the kitchen and the bar staff fill the sinks with ice. It's a fun run until last drinks with a hot mix of jamón croquetas, ice-cold Moritz beer from Barcelona and party-going punters. It becomes a place where relationships are made and broken. Eventually the window shutters come down, the deep-fryers are turned off, the punters wander off home or elsewhere and Marty and the crew huddle round for an end-of-the-week beer. Only for it all to start again first light on Monday.

FRIED CALAMARI BOCADILLOS

BOCADILLOS DE CALAMARES

	ALIOLI
1 X 600 G (1 LB 5 OZ) WHOLE CALAMARI	1 GARLIC CLOVE
SUNFLOWER OR OTHER MILD-FLAVOURED OIL, FOR DEEP-FRYING	SEA SALT FLAKES
SEA SALT FLAKES	1 EGG YOLK
2½ TABLESPOONS LEMON JUICE	2 TEASPOONS DIJON MUSTARD
100 G (3½ OZ) FINE SEMOLINA	75 ML (2⅓ FL OZ) EXTRA VIRGIN OLIVE OIL
⅓ CUP PARSLEY LEAVES, ROUGHLY CHOPPED	75 ML (2⅓ FL OZ) SUNFLOWER OR OTHER MILD-FLAVOURED OIL
12 BOCADILLOS (SEE PAGE 38)	1 TABLESPOON LEMON JUICE
6 GUINDILLAS (SEE GLOSSARY), DRAINED AND TORN IN HALF	

Take Madrid's calamari roll. It's a classic street food like our fish 'n' chips or meat pie. When treated with a bit of respect, this humble street snack is elevated into a completely different dish. We use a freshly baked, house-made bread roll, smother it with a generous dollop of alioli made with real, organic egg yolks. Then we layer up straight-from-the-fryer calamari and guindillas – spicy sweet pickled peppers. Now it becomes something truly great.

To make the alioli, place the garlic clove on a chopping board. Coarsely chop, then sprinkle with a pinch of salt and crush to a paste using the flat side of a heavy knife. Place a bowl on a folded damp tea (dish) towel. This will stop the bowl from moving around during whisking. Place the egg yolk, mustard and garlic paste in the bowl and gently combine using a balloon whisk. Combine the oils and, while whisking continuously, drizzle into the bowl, a few drops at a time. Each addition of oil needs to be emulsified into the egg yolk mixture before adding more. Continue whisking and slowly adding the oil until it is all used up. The alioli should gradually become thicker. Check for seasoning, then dissolve the appropriate amount of salt in the lemon juice and whisk into the alioli. Whisk in 2 teaspoons of warm water to stop the alioli from splitting. This makes 200 g (7 oz). Refrigerate the alioli, covered with plastic wrap touching the surface, for up to 3 days.

To clean the calamari, take a hold of its tentacles and pull them out of the hood. Cut the tentacles from the mouth and discard the mouth, cartilage and innards. Peel the skin from the hood and wings. Gently tear off the wings from the hood. Cut the cartilage from the wings and discard. Cut the hood in half along what appears to be a seam. Remove the clear quill and scrape away any remaining innards.

Separate the tentacles with a sharp knife and cut into 5 cm (2 inch) lengths. Cut the hood and wings into 5 cm x 5 mm (2 inch x ¼ inch) strips. Rinse the calamari pieces and drain well.

Heat the oil in a large heavy-based saucepan or deep-fryer to 180°C (350°F) or until a cube of bread dropped into the oil takes 15 seconds to turn golden.

Place the calamari in a bowl. Season with a good few pinches of salt, the lemon juice and sprinkle over the semolina. Mix well. Shake off the excess semolina and deep-fry the calamari for 1–1½ minutes or until lightly golden. Drain on paper towel. Season with salt and sprinkle with the parsley.

To serve, halve the rolls lengthways. Spread about 2 teaspoons of alioli over the bases, top with a piece of guindilla and some fried calamari. Sandwich with the tops and secure with a wooden skewer. Enjoy with an ice-cold beer.

SEVILLE ROLLS

150 G (5⅓ OZ) PIECE OF PORK BELLY, SKIN ON	1 CARROT, QUARTERED
1 X 150 G (5⅓ OZ) FRESH CHORIZO (SEE GLOSSARY)	80 G (2¾ OZ) PIECE OF JAMÓN (SEE GLOSSARY)
100 G (3½ OZ) PIECE OF BEEF SHIN	2 GARLIC CLOVES
1 X 250 G–300 G (9 OZ–10½ OZ) CHICKEN MARYLAND (LEG WITH THIGH ATTACHED)	12 BOCADILLOS (SEE PAGE 38)

Cocido is Spain's national dish of slow-cooked meats and vegetables. Being the national dish, it's always in plentiful supply, but what do you do when you have leftover cocido? Well, in Seville they serve it in a toasted roll. Our version is filled with slow-cooked jamón, beef and chicken and sandwiched in a press to make bite-sized pringás.

Place all the ingredients, except the bocadillos, in a sieve and rinse under cold running water to wash away any impurities. Drain well, then place in a pressure cooker with 1 litre (35 fl oz/4 cups) of water. Secure the lid and follow the manufacturer's instructions to bring up to pressure over medium–high heat. Once under pressure, which you'll know as it will be hissing from its valve, cook under pressure for 45 minutes or until the meat is tender. Alternatively, place the ingredients in a saucepan over medium–high heat, add 1 litre of cold water and cover. Bring to the boil, then simmer for 2–2½ hours or until the meat is tender.

Remove the meat and vegetables from the pressure cooker or saucepan and place in a bowl. When the meat is cool enough to handle, break the jamón up using your fingers. Remove the chicken meat from the bone and discard the bone and skin. Finely shred the chicken meat and other meat (pork belly, chorizo, beef shin) too, using your hands, into the bowl. Crush the carrot and garlic to a paste with the back of a fork and mix through the meats until roughly combined. Mix in a few tablespoons of the cooking liquid to moisten slightly and check the seasoning.

To serve, preheat a sandwich press to high. Halve the rolls lengthways and divide the filling between the bases. Sandwich with the tops and press down on each to close firmly. Toast for 6 minutes or until the bread is golden and the filling heated through. Enjoy with an ice-cold lager.

La Terraza is at the base of the headquarters of one of the nation's largest banks and it has quickly become lunchtime central. We found ourselves surrounded by people who demanded from us light, healthy food on a daily basis. The Spanish food we cook is based on the traditional food of the people of Spain. While we love the food from the bars in the barrios (neighbourhoods) of cities it's la cocina de los campesinos – the food of the people of the country – where our heart lies. This is the rustic fare of people working in the olive groves and fields, fare meant to sustain and fill. At La Terraza, we had to react quickly to meet the demands of our new clientele, people who used their brains more than their brawn. We thought long and hard and found that our traditional dishes, la cocina de los campesinos and its ingredients and flavour combinations, work just as well when given a lighter touch. While a Spaniard would never recognise these as their own dishes, the flavours are undeniably Spanish. This is the beauty of being an emigré operation – there are no rules, just possibilities.

ENSALADAS

SALADS

PIPIRRANA WITH RED & WHITE WITLOF

SERVES 8

ENDIVIAS CON PIPIRRANA

½ TWO-DAY-OLD BAGUETTE (SEE PAGES 38-9)

EXTRA VIRGIN OLIVE OIL, FOR DRIZZLING

1 GARLIC CLOVE, SKIN ON AND HALVED

4 RED WITLOF (BELGIUM ENDIVE)

4 WHITE WITLOF (BELGIUM ENDIVE)

PIPIRRANA

2 LEBANESE (SHORT) CUCUMBERS

3 TOMATOES, PEELED AND SEEDED
 (SEE GLOSSARY)

1 GREEN CAPSICUM (PEPPER), HALVED
 AND SEEDED

1 WHITE ONION

125 ML (4 FL OZ/½ CUP) EXTRA VIRGIN
 OLIVE OIL

60 ML (2 FL OZ/¼ CUP) SHERRY VINEGAR

SEA SALT FLAKES

1 TABLESPOON CUMIN SEEDS

Some Spanish dishes capture the spirit of the season perfectly. Pipirrana, for me, is summer. It's a bright blend of chopped ripe capsicum, cucumber, onion and garlic. Slightly sweet, it balances perfectly the bitterness of the witlof in this salad.

Preheat the oven to 180°C (350°F/Gas 4).

To make the pipirrana, partially peel the cucumbers, leaving a few strips of green skin. Halve lengthways, scoop out the seeds with a spoon and discard. Dice the cucumber, tomatoes, capsicum and onion into 5 mm (¼ inch) cubes. Place in a bowl with the olive oil and vinegar, season with salt and mix to combine.

Spread the cumin seeds evenly on a baking tray and roast for 5 minutes or until fragrant. Grind coarsely in a mortar and pestle or spice grinder and mix through the pipirrana. Set aside.

Thinly slice the baguette crossways into 24 x 2 mm (¹⁄₁₆ inch) thick slices. Lay the slices on baking trays, drizzle with a little olive oil and bake for 15 minutes or until crisp and lightly golden. Gently rub the croutons with the cut side of the garlic and sprinkle with a little salt. Break each into a few pieces. Set aside.

To serve, halve each witlof lengthways and spread the leaves open — so it looks like an abstract Sydney Opera House. Spoon over the pipirrana and scatter over the croûtons.

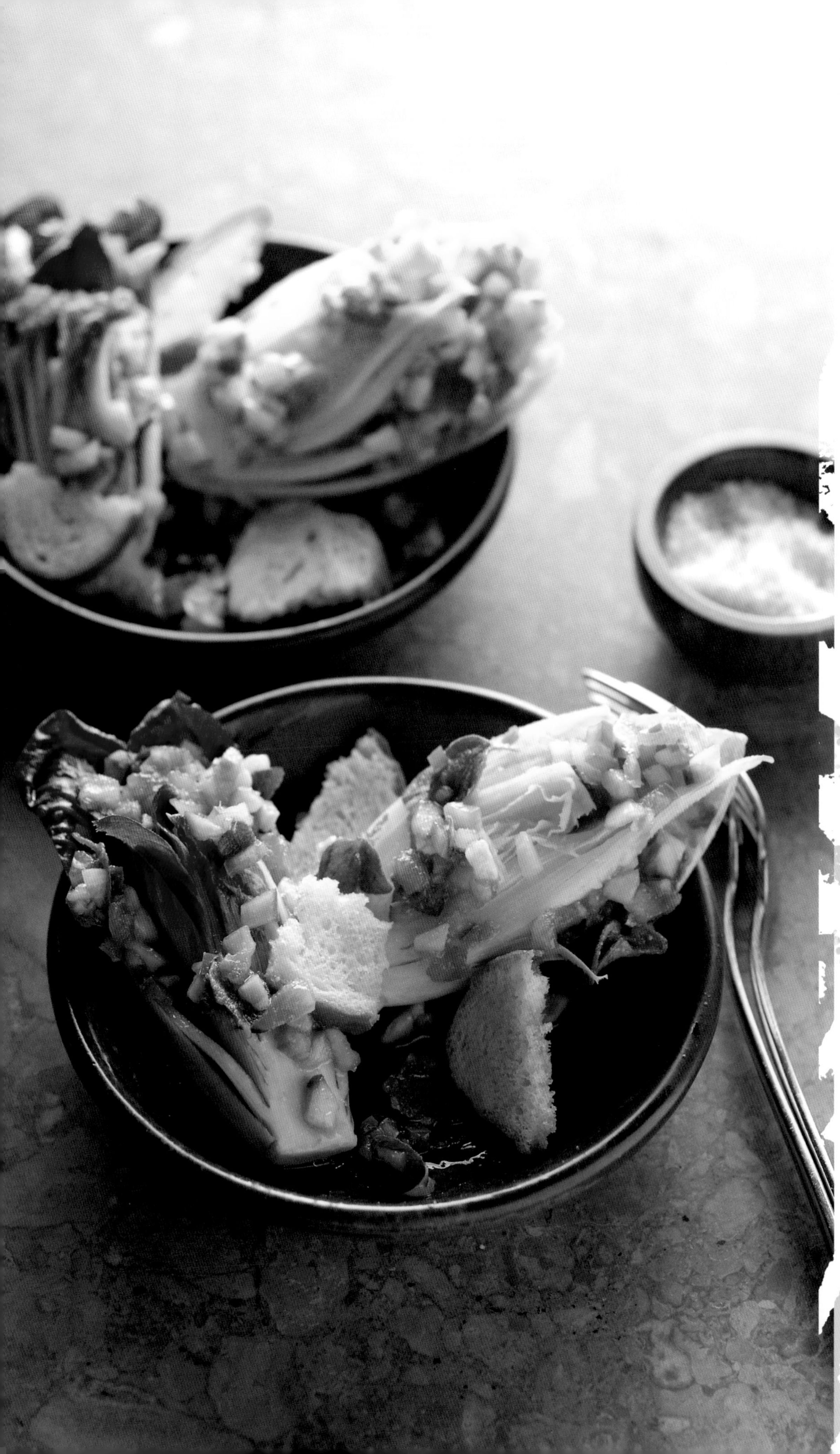

TOMATO SALAD WITH WHITE ANCHOVIES & PICKLED GARLIC

- 3 GREEN ZEBRA TOMATOES (SEE NOTE), PEELED (SEE GLOSSARY)
- 3 BLACK RUSSIAN TOMATOES (SEE NOTE), PEELED (SEE GLOSSARY)
- 1 OX HEART TOMATO
- 250 G (9 OZ) YELLOW CHERRY TOMATOES
- 250 G (9 OZ) CHERRY TOMATOES
- ½ FENNEL BULB
- 1 WHITE ONION
- 1 CUP TARRAGON LEAVES
- 16 GUINDILLAS (SEE GLOSSARY), DRAINED AND TORN IN HALF
- 2 TABLESPOONS CHARDONNAY VINEGAR
- 125 ML (4 FL OZ/½ CUP) EXTRA VIRGIN OLIVE OIL
- SEA SALT AND FRESHLY GROUND BLACK PEPPER
- 16 BOQUERONES (WHITE ANCHOVIES) (SEE GLOSSARY)
- 4 PICKLED GARLIC CLOVES (SEE GLOSSARY), DRAINED AND HALVED

SERVES 4
ENSALADA DE TOMATE CON BOQUERONES

This is an exercise in umami, the Japanese word for savoury. This is something Spanish cooks know how to achieve instinctively. Simply take the ripest tomatoes you can find, the best anchovies and Spanish pickled garlic and bring them together in a salad that appears uncomplicated but achieves true deliciousness.

Quarter the larger tomatoes and leave the small ones whole. Place in a large bowl.

Remove the woody stem of the fennel by cutting a V-shape at the base. Very thinly slice the fennel and add to the tomatoes. Halve the onion and very thinly slice. Add to the tomatoes with the tarragon and guindillas.

Drizzle over the vinegar and olive oil and season with salt and pepper. Gently toss the salad with your hands.

To serve, place the salad onto individual serving plates and top with the anchovies and pickled garlic. Spoon over any remaining dressing.

NOTE: Green zebra and black Russian tomatoes are available from specialty greengrocers. If a particular variety of tomato is not available, use whatever mix of ripe tomatoes you can find.

CURED SALMON WITH BLOOD ORANGE & ZUCCHINI

SERVES 10-12

ENSALADA DE SALMÓN CURADO

1 X 1 KG (2 LB 4 OZ) PIECE OF ATLANTIC SALMON FILLET, SKIN ON

60 G (2¼ OZ) FINE SEA SALT

1 TEASPOON FRESHLY GROUND BLACK PEPPER

140 G (5 OZ) SOFT BROWN SUGAR

1 TABLESPOON FENNEL SEEDS

½ SMALL FENNEL BULB, SHAVED

60 ML (2 FL OZ/¼ CUP) ANIS LIQUEUR (SEE NOTE)

4 ZUCCHINI (COURGETTES)

6 BLOOD ORANGES

100 ML (3½ FL OZ) EXTRA VIRGIN OLIVE OIL

100 G (3½ OZ/1 CUP) SEMI-DRIED BLACK OLIVES, PITTED

100 G (3½ OZ) PICKED WATERCRESS

FRESH HORSERADISH ROOT (OPTIONAL)

ORANGE GARNISH

1 ORANGE

2 TABLESPOONS ICING (CONFECTIONER'S) SUGAR

To cure a side of salmon yourself is a rewarding little process. In this recipe, we're cutting the intensity of the rich flesh with the fresh flavour of aniseed in various forms: a sweet Spanish anis liqueur, fennel seeds and shavings of crisp fresh fennel. Healthy and delicious.

You will need to begin this recipe 2 days ahead.

Run your fingers over the piece of salmon and, using a pair of fish tweezers, remove any protruding bones. Dip the tweezers into a small bowl of water to get the bones off. Pat the salmon dry with paper towel. Line a large tray with a double layer of plastic wrap, making sure there is enough overhang on the 2 long sides to easily wrap back over to cover the salmon. Place the salmon, skin-side down, on the plastic. Combine the salt, pepper, sugar, fennel seeds, shaved fennel and anis in a bowl. Massage the mixture into the salmon flesh. Make sure the entire surface of the flesh is covered in the mixture, then cover tightly with the plastic wrap. Refrigerate for 48 hours, turning every 12 hours.

To make the orange garnish, using a very sharp knife, slice the orange into 5 mm (¼ inch) thick rounds. Place on a dehydrator tray lined with baking paper and sprinkle with the icing sugar. Place in a food dehydrator at 64°C (147°F) and dry for 8 hours or until crisp. Alternatively, place on a wire rack on a baking tray, sprinkle with the sugar and dry in a non fan-forced oven on the lowest temperature with the door ajar for 8 hours or until crisp. The time and results will vary from oven to oven. Store in an airtight container for up to 2 days.

To serve, remove the salmon from the plastic wrap and allow any liquid to drain away. Brush off the curing mixture and pat the salmon dry with paper towel. Starting at the wider end, cut the salmon crossways into 2 mm (¹⁄₁₆ inch) thick slices, cutting straight down not on an angle. Place in a large bowl.

Using a sharp knife or mandolin, very thinly slice the zucchini lengthways. Add to the salmon.

Peel 4 oranges and slice into 5 mm (¼ inch) thick rounds. Add to the salmon with the olives. Mix gently.

Juice the remaining oranges. Combine the juice with the olive oil and a good pinch of salt to make a dressing.

Divide the salmon mixture between plates, garnish with the watercress and orange garnish and drizzle over some of the dressing. Finely grate over some horseradish to add a nice kick.

NOTE: Anis liqueur (licor de anís) is a clear, colourless, aniseed-flavoured liqueur. It is consumed in Spain as a pick-me-up on a cold morning, or as a little shot throughout the day. Its strong liquorice-like flavour makes it popular in the kitchen in sweet dishes. If you can't find it, try Pernod or something similar.

AIR-DRIED TUNA WITH PRICKLY PEAR

SERVES 4–6

MOJAMA CON HIGOS INDIOS

100 G (3½ OZ) BLANCHED ALMONDS

SEA SALT FLAKES

1 TEASPOON SMOKED SWEET PAPRIKA
 (PIMENTÓN)

4 PRICKLY PEARS (SEE NOTE)

12 PIMIENTOS DE PIQUILLO (SEE GLOSSARY),
 DRAINED

20 THIN SLICES MOJAMA (SEE NOTE)

EXTRA VIRGIN OLIVE OIL, FOR DRIZZLING

Mojama is air-dried tuna, the jamón of the sea world. For generations, almonds and mojama have been served together. To achieve a salty-flesh-and-sweet dimension, we have added prickly pear to the plate and it's as if these ingredients were already married. A simple little threesome. Enjoy with a glass of ice-cold manzanilla.

Preheat the oven to 180°C (350°F/Gas 4). Spread the almonds on a baking tray and lightly roast for 10 minutes. Remove from the oven, sprinkle with salt and paprika and toss gently to coat.

Meanwhile, prepare the prickly pears. These are covered in clusters of nasty tiny spikes so wear thick rubber gloves when handling. Peel with a sharp knife to remove the skin and remove any errant spikes. The spikes get into everything so wash the chopping board well and wipe down the bench before continuing. Cut the flesh into 5 mm (¼ inch) thick rounds.

Cut the peppers at the seams and open out to form flat triangular pieces.

To serve, place the pimientos on one half of a serving plate and place the mojama on the other half. Arrange the prickly pear over the top. Sprinkle with a line of almonds and drizzle with the olive oil. Serve straight away as the juices of the prickly pear will dissolve the mojama.

NOTE: Prickly pear is in season during spring. If it's not available, substitute a ripe melon, whichever is the nicest looking. Mojama is available from Spanish grocers and some good food stores.

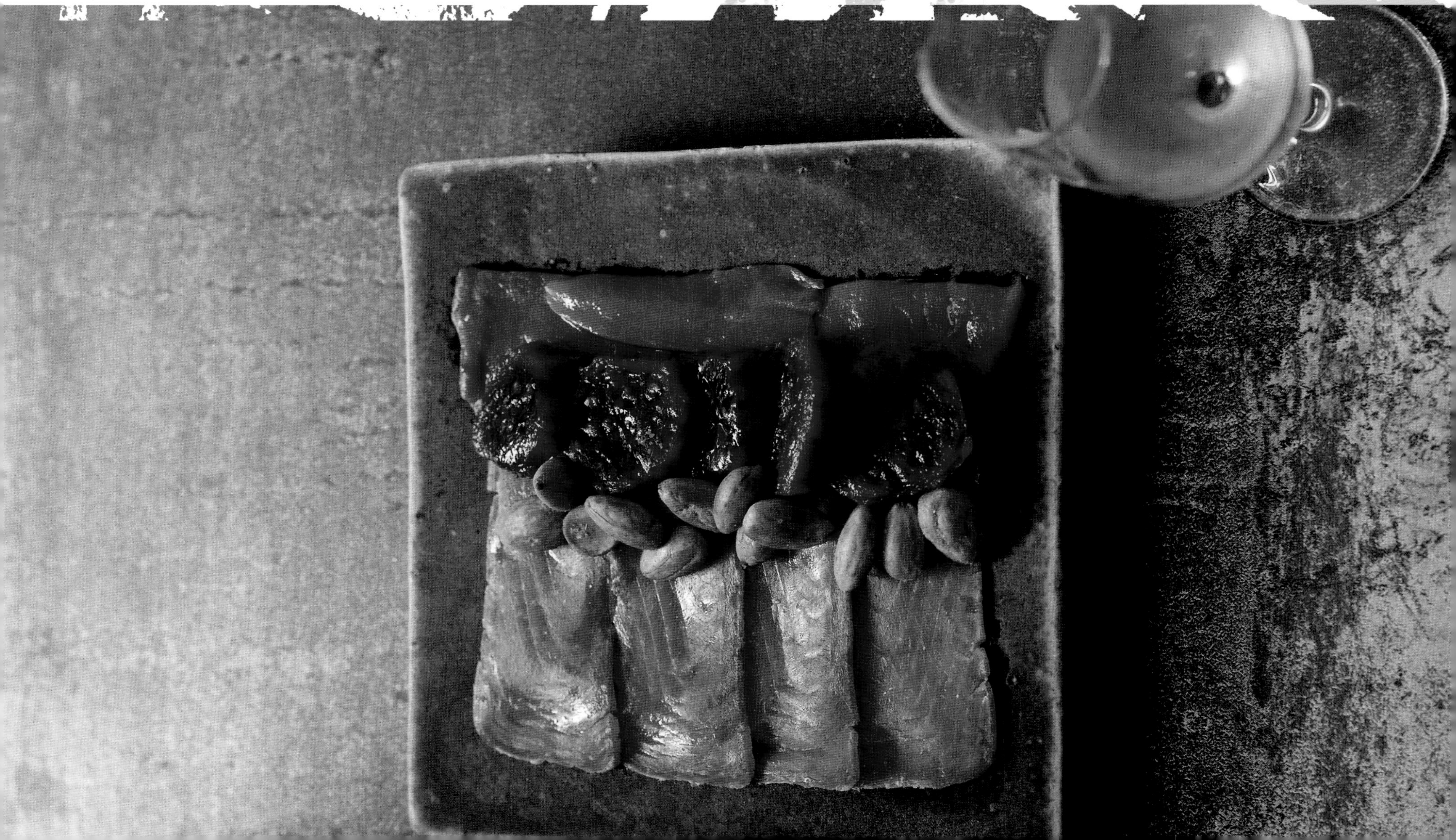

POTATO SALAD WITH ALIOLI, PICKLED GARLIC & PALITOS DE PAN

300 G (10½ OZ) ROCK SALT

1.5 KG (3 LB 5 OZ/ABOUT 6) WHITE-SKINNED
   POTATOES, WASHED AND UNPEELED

2 WHITE ONIONS, FINELY DICED

SEA SALT AND FRESHLY GROUND BLACK
   PEPPER

2 GARLIC CLOVES

270 G (9½ OZ/1 CUP) ALIOLI (SEE PAGE 54)
   (YOU WILL NEED TO MAKE ABOUT
   1½ TIMES THE RECIPE)

1 SMALL BUNCH CHIVES, FINELY CHOPPED

2 TABLESPOONS FINELY CHOPPED PARSLEY

18 PICKLED GARLIC CLOVES (SEE GLOSSARY),
   DRAINED

250 G (9 OZ) PALITOS DE PAN OR GRISSINI,
   BROKEN INTO 8 CM (3¼ INCH) LENGTHS

SERVES 6

ENSALADA DE PATATAS ALIÑADAS

Palitos de pan are like grissini, only shorter. They're served with meals like bread. Here we're using them as little scoops to pick up a rich garlicky potato salad, a real crowd pleaser.

Preheat the oven to 180°C (350°F/Gas 4). Spread the rock salt evenly over a baking tray and place the potatoes on top. The salt helps to draw out excess moisture from the potatoes. Bake for 45 minutes or until the potatoes are cooked through. Allow to cool just enough to handle. Using a sharp knife, peel the potatoes and dice into 1 cm (½ inch) cubes and place in a bowl. Add half of the onion, season with salt and pepper and mix together. Stand for a few minutes to allow the residual heat from the potato to soften the onion.

Place the garlic cloves on a chopping board. Coarsely chop, then sprinkle with a pinch of salt and crush to a paste using the flat side of a heavy knife. Combine with the alioli, chives, parsley and remaining onion. Add to the potato mixture and toss to combine. Season with pepper.

To serve, place the potato salad in individual serving bowls, garnish with 3 pickled garlic cloves and insert several palitos pieces into the salad. Serve straight away.

NOTE: If you want to make this salad ahead of time, make sure you have a little extra alioli on hand to mix through just before serving as the potato will soak up some of the dressing as it sits. Refrigerate the salad until ready to serve.

WARM BEETROOT & SHALLOT SALAD WITH FRESH CURD

SERVES 4-6

ENSALADA DE REMOLACHA

4 BUNCHES (ABOUT 500 G/1 LB 2 OZ) BABY
  BEETROOT (BEETS)
1 TABLESPOON WHITE WINE VINEGAR
45 ML (1½ FL OZ) EXTRA VIRGIN OLIVE OIL,
  PLUS EXTRA FOR DRIZZLING
15 FRENCH SHALLOTS (ESCHALOTS), TRIMMED
2½ TABLESPOONS CHARDONNAY VINEGAR
1 TABLESPOON HONEY

FINELY GRATED ZEST AND JUICE OF 1 LEMON
¼ CUP MINT LEAVES, CHOPPED
SEA SALT FLAKES

CURD
1 LITRE (35 FL OZ/4 CUPS) MILK
1 ML (⅟₃₂ FL OZ) RENNET (SEE GLOSSARY)

Chef Marty at La Terraza describes this sweet earthy salad with his straight-to-the-point attitude. "My lady customers love it," he says, "because it's healthy and because it looks beautiful. As long as they don't spill it on their suits." We concur.

To make the curd, heat the milk in a small saucepan over very low heat to 38°C (100°F). Use a digital thermometer with a probe to ensure the temperature is spot on or the curds will not form properly. Remove from the heat and add the rennet. After 8 minutes the whey should have separated and delicate white curds should have formed. Gently spoon the curd into a fine sieve placed over a bowl. Refrigerate for 1 hour to drain off any excess liquid.

Cut the stalks from the beetroot, leaving about 1 cm (½ inch) attached. Place in a large saucepan, cover with cold water and add the white wine vinegar. Place over high heat and bring to the boil. Reduce the heat to medium–low and simmer for 45 minutes or until tender. Remove from the heat and leave to cool in the cooking liquid. Drain well. Peel the beetroot and discard the skin. Cut any larger beetroot in half. Set aside.

Heat the olive oil in a deep-sided frying pan over low heat. Cook the shallots for 5 minutes or until caramelised. Add the chardonnay vinegar, honey, lemon juice and zest and 250 ml (9 fl oz/1 cup) of water and stir. Add the beetroot and cook, stirring occasionally, for 45 minutes or until the liquid thickens enough to lightly glaze the beetroot. Remove from the heat and cool to room temperature. Fold the mint through the beetroot. Check the seasoning.

To serve, spoon the beetroot and shallots onto a serving plate. Crumble over the curd, sprinkle with salt and drizzle with a little oil.

CATALAN WILTED SPINACH

80 G (2¾ OZ/½ CUP) PINE NUTS	125 ML (4 FL OZ/½ CUP) EXTRA VIRGIN OLIVE OIL
500 G (1 LB 2 OZ) BABY SPINACH LEAVES	2 GARLIC CLOVES, THINLY SLICED
120 G (4¼ OZ/⅔ CUP) RAISINS	2½ TABLESPOONS LEMON JUICE
200 ML (7 FL OZ) PEDRO XIMÉNEZ SHERRY	SEA SALT FLAKES
(SEE GLOSSARY)	

SERVES 6

ESPINACAS A LA CATALANA

This is a contemporary twist on a Catalan classic. Flavour hot olive oil with garlic, then pour it over spinach leaves. The heat wilts the spinach and the few sherry-soaked raisins.

Preheat the oven to 180°C (350°F/Gas 4). Place the pine nuts on a baking tray lined with baking paper and roast for 5 minutes or until lightly golden.

Wash and dry the spinach and set aside in a large stainless steel bowl. Soak the raisins in the sherry in a small bowl.

Heat the olive oil in a frying pan over medium heat. Add the garlic and cook, stirring regularly, for 2–3 minutes or until golden.

Pour the hot oil and garlic over the spinach and mix well with tongs. Add the raisin mixture and lemon juice and season with salt. Toss to combine. Set aside for 15 minutes, tossing the dressing through the leaves every 5 minutes. Check the seasoning and serve.

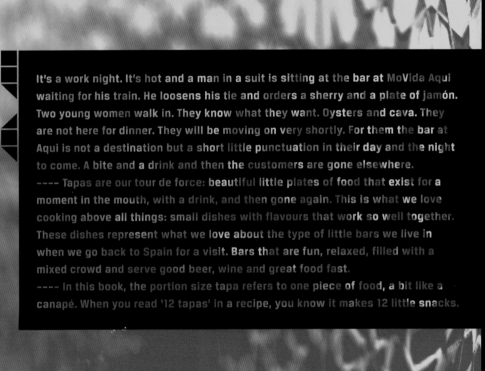

It's a work night. It's hot and a man in a suit is sitting at the bar at MoVida Aqui waiting for his train. He loosens his tie and orders a sherry and a plate of jamón. Two young women walk in. They know what they want. Oysters and cava. They are not here for dinner. They will be moving on very shortly. For them the bar at Aqui is not a destination but a short little punctuation in their day and the night to come. A bite and a drink and then the customers are gone elsewhere.

---- Tapas are our tour de force: beautiful little plates of food that exist for a moment in the mouth, with a drink, and then gone again. This is what we love cooking above all things: small dishes with flavours that work so well together. These dishes represent what we love about the type of little bars we live in when we go back to Spain for a visit. Bars that are fun, relaxed, filled with a mixed crowd and serve good beer, wine and great food fast.

---- In this book, the portion size tapa refers to one piece of food, a bit like a canapé. When you read '12 tapas' in a recipe, you know it makes 12 little snacks.

TAPAS

BAR FOOD

POTATO CRISPS WITH LEMON SALT

SERVES 4

PATATAS FRITAS CON LIMON

4 SEBAGO POTATOES, UNPEELED

SUNFLOWER OR OTHER MILD-FLAVOURED OIL, FOR DEEP-FRYING

LEMON SALT

FINELY GRATED ZEST OF 1 LEMON

1 TEASPOON CASTER (SUPERFINE) SUGAR

1¼ TABLESPOONS FINE SEA SALT FLAKES

On hot nights, when the after-work crowd comes in at MoVida Aqui, the boys in the bar pour the guests an ice-cold beer and, in true Andalusian style, tear off a square of wax paper, lay it on the bar and upend a bowl of crisps. With a salty citrus tang, these are no ordinary potato chips.

To make the lemon salt, combine the lemon zest and sugar and spread on a dehydrator tray lined with baking paper. Place in a food dehydrator at 57°C (135°F) and dry for 12 hours. Alternatively spread on a baking tray lined with baking paper and dry in a non fan-forced oven at the lowest temperature with the door ajar until the zest feels like desiccated coconut and crumbles easily. The time will vary from oven to oven but it should take about 6 hours. Grind the mixture with a mortar and pestle with the salt until finely ground and pale yellow.

Using a sharp knife or mandolin, cut the potatoes crossways into 1 mm (1/32 inch) thick slices. Using a 6 cm (2½ inch) round biscuit cutter, stamp out a round from each slice. Discard the trimmings (you can fry them up and eat them too, but they just don't look as good!). Soak the potato rounds in cold water for 10 minutes to remove the starch. Drain and pat completely dry.

Fill a large heavy-based saucepan or deep-fryer one-third full with oil and heat to 170°C (325°F) or until a cube of bread dropped into the oil takes 20 seconds to turn golden. Deep-fry the potato rounds, in batches, for 2 minutes, turning regularly, until golden. Drain on paper towel and season with the lemon salt.

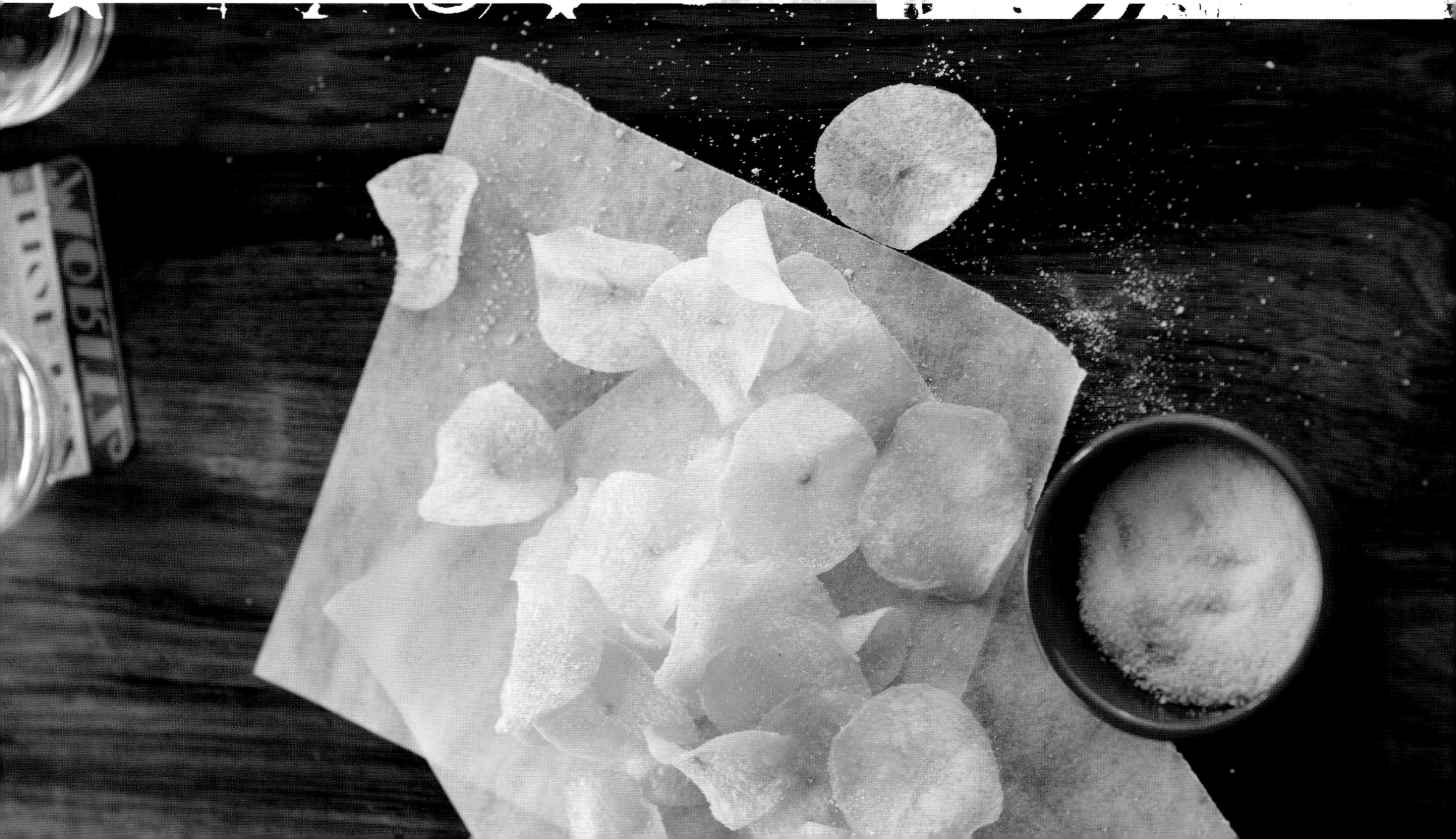

SMOKED EEL CROQUETTES WITH HORSERADISH

1 X 800 G (1 LB 12 OZ) SMOKED EEL

200 G (7 OZ) UNSALTED BUTTER

1 LARGE BROWN ONION, FINELY DICED

325 G (11½ OZ) PLAIN (ALL-PURPOSE) FLOUR,
   PLUS EXTRA FOR DUSTING

2½ TEASPOONS CORNFLOUR (CORNSTARCH)

750 ML (26 FL OZ/3 CUPS) MILK

200 G (7 OZ) QUESO DE MAHÓN
   (SEE GLOSSARY), FINELY GRATED

3 TEASPOONS COOKING SALT

2 TABLESPOONS STORE-BOUGHT
   HORSERADISH CREAM

3 EGGS, LIGHTLY BEATEN

150 G (5⅓ OZ) PANKO (JAPANESE)
   BREADCRUMBS

SUNFLOWER OIL, FOR DEEP-FRYING

SEA SALT FLAKES

24 TAPAS
CROQUETAS DE ANGUILAS

The key to a good croquette is the béchamel sauce. It has to be silky smooth when you bite into the croquette. This means you need to make a beautiful viscous béchamel to start with, not too runny and not too thick. This béchamel base works just as well with chopped jamón, mushroom duxelle or cooked-down leeks.

You will need to begin this recipe the day before.

Using your fingers, peel the skin from the eel and discard; it will come away easily. Remove and discard the bones. Cut the flesh into 5 mm (¼ inch) dice, checking there are no stray bones. Set aside.

Melt the butter in a large heavy-based saucepan over medium–low heat. Add the onion and cook for 8 minutes or until soft and translucent but do not let it brown. Add 175 g (6 oz) of the flour and all the cornflour to the pan and cook, stirring continuously, for 3 minutes. Add the milk, 185 ml (6 fl oz/¾ cup) at a time, stirring continuously and vigorously and scraping the base of the pan with a wooden spoon. This should prevent lumps from forming. The mixture will thicken quickly. Before the last addition of milk, mix in the eel, Mahón, horseradish cream and salt. Gradually add the remaining milk, a little at a time, stirring continuously. Continue cooking, stirring occasionally, for 15 minutes to thicken and cook out the flour. Pour into a shallow tray, cover with baking paper and allow to cool, then refrigerate overnight. This will make the mixture firm enough to handle.

The next day, make the croquettes. Take 2 heaped teaspoons of the mixture at a time and form into oval shapes, about 7 cm x 3 cm (2¾ x 1¼ inches).

Arrange 3 plates with a lip or wide shallow bowls in a row. Place the remaining flour in the first, the beaten egg in the second and the breadcrumbs in the third. Roll the croquettes in the flour, dip in the egg, allowing the excess to drain off, then roll in the breadcrumbs, coating well. Place on a tray, cover with plastic wrap and refrigerate for 3 hours or until firm and chilled.

Fill a large heavy-based saucepan or deep-fryer one-third full with oil and heat to 180°C (350°F) or until a cube of bread dropped into the oil takes 15 seconds to turn golden. Deep-fry the croquettes, in batches, for 3–4 minutes or until golden all over. Drain on paper towel. Sprinkle with salt and serve straight away.

FRESHLY SHUCKED OYSTERS WITH CAVA DRESSING

12 TAPAS

OSTRAS

200 ML (7 FL OZ) ROSÉ CAVA OR OTHER SPARKLING PINK WINE	12 OYSTERS, UNSHUCKED
1 SPRIG THYME	EXTRA VIRGIN OLIVE OIL, FOR DRIZZLING
30 G (1 OZ) CASTER (SUPERFINE) SUGAR	**SALT BED**
2 X 2 G (¹⁄₁₆ OZ) GELATINE SHEETS (GOLD-STRENGTH)	250 G (9 OZ) ROCK SALT
	250 G (9 OZ) FINE SEA SALT

While there's more than one way to open an oyster, there's only one way in our kitchen and that's to come in from the rear of the shell. Here Chef Jimmy (see page 166) of MoVida Next Door gives a step-by-step description on how to open oysters. Learn to open an oyster properly and you have a skill for life.

Place the cava, thyme and sugar in a small saucepan over medium heat and stir for 1 minute or until the sugar dissolves, then remove from the heat and allow to cool slightly. Remove the thyme sprig and discard.

Place the gelatine sheets in 200 ml (7 fl oz) of cold water and leave for 2 minutes or until softened. Squeeze out the excess water. Add the gelatine to the warm cava mixture and whisk until dissolved. Strain through a fine sieve into a small 18 cm x 13 cm (7 inch x 5 inch) shallow plastic container. Cover with plastic wrap and refrigerate for 3 hours or overnight.

To make the salt bed, combine the rock and fine salt with 80 ml (2½ fl oz/⅓ cup) of water in a bowl. Place the mixture on a large serving plate or 12 individual plates to make a thick bed for the oysters. Set aside.

To shuck the oysters, wash the outside of the oysters and scrub off any sand or algae. Take an oyster shucker in one hand and wrap a folded tea (dish) towel around the other hand to protect it. Place an oyster, flat-side up with the hinge (the pointy end) facing your hand holding the shucker. Insert the tip of the shucker at a shallow angle in the hinge between the two shells and wiggle until it finds a little pocket just to one side of the hinge. Push the blade in between the two halves until the tip is just inside, then gently twist the shucker to lever open the shell. Run the shucker under the inside of the top shell to release the muscle (adductor). Remove and discard the top shell. Run the shucker around the oyster where it is attached to the bottom shell to cut the muscle. Pick out any small pieces of shell but do not rinse the oyster. Place the oyster on the salt bed. Repeat with the remaining oysters.

To serve, scramble the cava jelly using a fork until it resembles crushed ice. Spoon a little jelly over each oyster, drizzle over a little olive oil and enjoy with a chilled glass of cava.

ROBBO
MOVIDA

There's something about Chef Robbo's bottom jaw. Square and solid, sometimes it hangs from his head in amazement, sometimes in disbelief, but when something amusing happens, his whole face erupts in a mischievous smile. With his laconic Aussie drawl, Chef Robbo has a sense of humour so dry you don't know whether he's having a go at you or having a joke. Sometimes there's a bit of both.

---- He's now head chef at MoVida Hosier Lane, our oldest restaurant in a graffiti-covered cobbled lane near the Cathedral in the heart of Melbourne. He's a suburban lad who worked in pub kitchens before he came to us. Through sheer motivation he's worked his way to the top. Great chefs continue to grow and learn as they get older. Chef Robbo is always reading, buying cookbooks and industry magazines from overseas and trawling the net for new techniques. Whenever his mates return from Madrid Fusión – an annual global molecular cuisine conference – he's instantly on the phone asking them about the new techniques they've seen.

---- The food he sends out always blows me away. Chef Robbo has a great sense of order and symmetry and many of his dishes reflect that – they are petite and precise. But then he'll embrace the essence of comida rustica – the rustic food, often from poorer times, that is one of the bedrocks of Spanish cooking – in his slow-cooked estofado or in the simple way he handles fish. He takes what other chefs at MoVida have made before him and uses those recipes as building blocks for his own dishes, using the culture of cooking we have built up in our kitchens, and then showing us something new about what we have always done.

PORK CRACKLING

10-12 TAPAS

CORTEZAS
DE CERDO

1 KG (2 LB 4 OZ) PORK SKIN (SEE NOTE)
SUNFLOWER OIL, FOR DEEP-FRYING
SEA SALT FLAKES

Ever wanted to know how to make pork crackling? Well, the Madrileños perfected the recipe years ago. It is truly simple – it just takes a little time. Serve in a bowl when guests drop in and enjoy with a cold beer or glass of sherry.

You will need to begin this recipe 2 days ahead.

Place the pork skin in a large saucepan, cover with water and bring to the boil over high heat. Reduce the heat to medium–low and simmer for 2 hours or until soft. Drain and place, skin-side down, on a tray lined with baking paper. Cover with more baking paper, place another tray on top and weigh it down with food cans or a heavy container to flatten the skin. Refrigerate for 3 hours or until chilled.

Remove the food cans, tray and paper from the skin. Using a spoon, scrape all of the fat away from the skin. Place on a dehydrator tray lined with baking paper. Place in a food dehydrator at 65°C (149°F) and dry for 32 hours. Alternatively, place on a baking tray lined with baking paper and dry in a non fan-forced oven at the lowest temperature with the door ajar. The time will vary from oven to oven but it should take about 8 hours or overnight. It should be hard and look like plastic. You can store the dried pork skin for up to 2 days in an airtight container.

To cook, fill a large heavy-based saucepan or deep-fryer one-third full with oil and heat to 180°C (350°F) or until a cube of bread dropped into the oil takes 15 seconds to turn golden. Break the skin into about 3 cm (1¼ inch) pieces and deep-fry, in batches, for 20–30 seconds. The skin will puff up and dramatically increase in size. Drain on paper towel. Season with salt and serve straight away.

NOTE: Pork skin is available from butchers but you may need to order it in advance. Sometimes you can find it, labelled as pork crackling, in the fresh meat section of supermarkets.

MORITZ

DUCK CONSOMMÉ WITH PORK CRACKLING & DUCK JAMÓN

12 TAPAS

CALDO CON CORTEZA DE CERDO Y JAMÓN DE PATO

4 DUCK CARCASSES (SEE NOTES)	6 BAY LEAVES
250 ML (9 FL OZ/1 CUP) BRANDY	½ BUNCH THYME
250 ML (9 FL OZ/1 CUP) RED WINE	4 STAR ANISE
2 TABLESPOONS EXTRA VIRGIN OLIVE OIL	160 ML (5¼ FL OZ) PEDRO XIMÉNEZ SHERRY (SEE GLOSSARY)
4 CARROTS, ROUGHLY DICED	
4 BROWN ONIONS, ROUGHLY DICED	CORTEZAS DE CERDO (SEE PAGE 92)
4 GARLIC BULBS, HALVED	60 SLICES DUCK JAMÓN (SEE NOTES)

I love caldo – a clear broth sometimes served in bars as a pre-alcoholic pick-me-up. This delicately spiced duck consommé is given a salty meaty hit with a few slices of duck jamón and the pork crackling adds some crunch. Chef James of MoVida Aqui uses a modern 'freeze-and-thaw' method to clarify the stock.

Preheat the oven to 220°C (425°F/Gas 7). Place the duck carcasses in 2 flameproof roasting trays and roast for 30 minutes or until golden, swapping the trays from the top to the bottom racks halfway through cooking. Remove from the oven. Strain off the duck fat and discard or reserve for another use (see notes). Set the carcasses aside.

Combine the brandy and wine and pour half into each tray. Simmer over medium heat to deglaze, scraping the dark cooked-on bits from the bases. Set aside.

Heat the oil in a pressure cooker over medium–high heat. Add the carrot, onion, garlic, bay leaves, thyme and star anise and cook, stirring regularly, for 35 minutes or until the onion and carrot are golden.

Pour in the brandy and wine mixture. Remove half of the vegetables and set aside.

Add 2 duck carcasses to the remaining vegetables in the pressure cooker. Add 5 litres (175 fl oz) of cold water. Secure the lid and follow the manufacturer's instructions to bring to pressure over high heat. Once under pressure, which you'll know as it will be hissing from its valve, reduce the heat to medium and cook under pressure for 30 minutes. Strain over a bowl, discarding the solids.

Return the liquid to the pressure cooker with the remaining vegetables and duck carcasses and repeat cooking under pressure. Strain over a bowl, discarding the solids. You should now have about 3.5 litres (122½ fl oz) of duck stock.

If you don't have a pressure cooker, use the same process but simmer in a large saucepan for 4 hours. You can do this all in one batch if you have a big enough saucepan. Allow to cool, then place in a large, deep-sided tray and freeze overnight. It's important to make the stock in 2 batches if using a pressure cooker as they should never be overfilled.

94

The next day, remove the fat from the top of the stock with a spoon. Briefly dip the base of the tray in hot water to help loosen the stock, then turn out onto a bench. Wrap the block of stock in a double layer of muslin (cheesecloth) and place on a large wire rack placed inside a large deep-sided tray. Allow to defrost in the fridge for 6–8 hours. As the stock defrosts, a pure clear liquid will drip into the tray, while the impurities remain with the jellied stock trapped by the muslin. Discard the remaining jellied stock.

Pour the liquid into a saucepan with the sherry and place over medium heat. Heat until hot but not boiling, then remove from the heat and allow to cool slightly.

To serve, divide the consommé between glasses and place on serving plates with a large piece of corteza de cerdo and 5 slices of duck jamón.

NOTES: Duck carcasses are available from poultry specialists and butchers but may need to be ordered in advance. Duck fat is great for roasting potatoes.

Duck jamón is available from select gourmet delicatessens. If unavailable, substitute with 24 slices of jamón serrano.

For cocktail parties, the consommé can be served in shot glasses; in which case, the recipe makes enough for about 18.

BLUE CHEESE SANDWICHES

12 TAPAS

BOCADILLOS DE QUESO DE VALDEÓN

FILO CRACKERS

4 SHEETS FILO PASTRY

MILK, FOR BRUSHING

CASTER (SUPERFINE) SUGAR, FOR SPRINKLING

BLUE CHEESE CREAM

85 G (3 OZ) QUESO DE VALDEÓN (SEE GLOSSARY) OR OTHER CREAMY, FULL-FLAVOURED BLUE CHEESE

110 ML (3¾ FL OZ) POURING (SINGLE) CREAM

SEA SALT AND FRESHLY GROUND BLACK PEPPER

This is a dish from Spain's Chef Marcos Morán from Casa Gerardo in Asturias. He and his dad run a restaurant that has been serving classic Asturian dishes, such as fabada, a rich bean and sausage stew, since 1882. This blue cheese cream and cracker snack is one of Marco's modern inventions.

To make the filo crackers, preheat the oven to 165°C (320°F/Gas 2–3). Keep the filo pastry covered with a damp tea (dish) towel. Place a sheet of filo on a bench, brush with a little milk and sprinkle very lightly with sugar. Top with a second sheet of filo and repeat brushing and sprinkling. Repeat once more, then top with the final sheet of filo but do not brush or sprinkle. Cut into 24 even-sized squares and place on a large tray lined with baking paper. Cover with more baking paper and place another tray on top to weight down the filo and stop it from buckling during cooking. Bake for 12 minutes or until crisp and lightly golden. Remove the top tray and allow the crackers to cool on the tray. (These can be stored in an airtight container for up to 3 days.)

Meanwhile, make the blue cheese cream. Crumble the queso de Valdeón into a bowl. Add the cream and mash together until thick and smooth. Check the seasoning. Cover and refrigerate until ready to use.

To serve, arrange 12 filo crackers on a bench and spoon about 1 tablespoon of the cheese mixture onto one-half of each cracker. Take another cracker and place on top of the mixture to make an A-shape. Stand the crackers upright on a serving platter. To eat, grasp at the join and slowly squash the crackers together to make a sandwich.

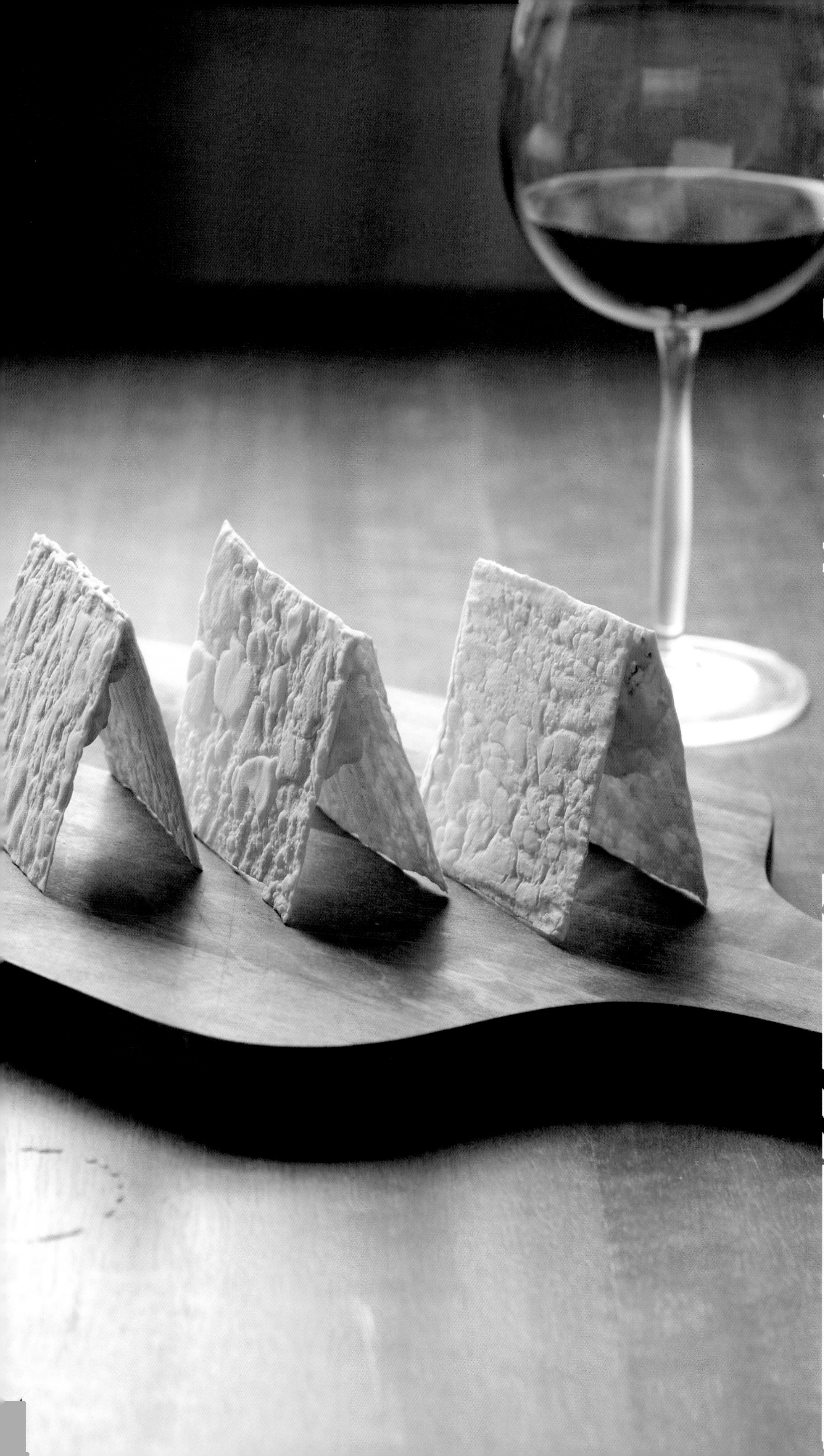

SCOTCH EGGS

12 TAPAS

HUEVOS ESCOSESES

12 QUAIL EGGS, AT ROOM TEMPERATURE	**BACALAO CASING**
60 ML (2 FL OZ/¼ CUP) WHITE WINE VINEGAR	2 TABLESPOONS EXTRA VIRGIN OLIVE OIL
2 EGGS, LIGHTLY BEATEN	1 BROWN ONION, FINELY DICED
100 G (3½ OZ/⅔ CUP) PLAIN	2 GARLIC CLOVES, THINLY SLICED
(ALL-PURPOSE) FLOUR	1 BAY LEAF
100 G (3½ OZ/1¼ CUPS) PANKO (JAPANESE)	200 G (7 OZ) DESALINATED REHYDRATED
BREADCRUMBS (SEE NOTE)	BACALAO (SEE GLOSSARY), SHREDDED
SUNFLOWER OR OLIVE OIL, FOR DEEP-FRYING	160 G (5¾ OZ/ABOUT 1) FLOURY POTATO,
SEA SALT FLAKES	SUCH AS RUSSET
¼ QUANTITY (100 G/3½ OZ) ALIOLI	250 ML (9 FL OZ/1 CUP) POURING (SINGLE)
(SEE PAGE 54), FOR DIPPING	CREAM
	1 TABLESPOON LEMON JUICE

When Chef Ewan was working in the UK he started thinking about ways to improve the classic scotch egg. The Brits wouldn't have a bar of it, so when he came to work with us at MoVida Aqui he found a team with an open mind: he encased a creamy quail egg in a blanket of bacalao and a crust of golden panko breadcrumbs. We think he has created a new classic.

You will need to begin this recipe the day before.

To make the bacalao casing, heat the oil in a heavy-based saucepan over medium-low heat and sauté the onion, garlic and bay leaves for 8 minutes or until the onion is soft. Reduce the heat to low, add the bacalao and cook for 5 minutes or until heated through.

Meanwhile, peel the potato and cut into large even squares. Place in a small saucepan, cover with water and bring to the boil over high heat. Reduce the heat to medium–low and simmer for 12 minutes or until tender. Drain well. Return the potato to the pan over low heat, add the bacalao mixture and cream and mix well. Cook for 15 minutes or until the cream is absorbed. Transfer to a food processor with the lemon juice and process for 4 minutes or until smooth. Check the seasoning and allow to cool. Transfer to an airtight container and refrigerate overnight.

Meanwhile, pierce the base of each egg with a pin — this will make them easier to peel later on. Bring 750 ml (26 fl oz/3 cups) of water and the vinegar to the boil over medium heat, then reduce to a simmer. Carefully add the eggs and cook for 2 minutes 15 seconds. Remove and refresh in iced water for 10 minutes. Carefully peel the eggs, as the yolks will still be very runny, place in an airtight container and refrigerate overnight.

The next day, assemble the scotch eggs. Take 1 heaped tablespoon (about 30 g/1 oz) of the salt cod casing and flatten between the palms of your hands into a 1 cm (½ inch) thick, 6 cm–7 cm (2½ inch–2¾ inch) round patty. Place a quail egg in the centre of the patty and carefully wrap the bacalao around the egg to enclose completely. Place on a tray. Repeat with the remaining eggs and bacalao casing. Refrigerate for 1 hour to firm up a little.

Arrange 3 plates with a lip or wide shallow bowls in a row. Place the flour in the first, the beaten egg in the second and the breadcrumbs in the third. Roll the encased eggs in the flour, dip in the beaten egg, allowing the excess to drain off, then roll in the breadcrumbs, coating well, and place on a tray. Refrigerate for at least 1 hour or until ready to serve.

Fill a large heavy-based saucepan or deep-fryer one-third full with oil and heat to 170°C (325°F) or until a cube of bread dropped into the oil takes 20 seconds to turn golden. Deep-fry the scotch eggs, in batches, for 3 minutes or until golden all over. Drain on paper towel.

To serve, sprinkle with salt and serve with alioli.

NOTE: Panko breadcrumbs are available from Asian grocers and good food stores.

VIEIRAS $16...
GAMBAS $16...
PESCAD...

CEVICHE SCALLOPS

3 GARLIC SHOOTS (SEE NOTE)

150 ML (5 FL OZ) CHARDONNAY VINEGAR

½ TEASPOON FINE SEA SALT FLAKES

1 TEASPOON CASTER (SUPERFINE) SUGAR

2½ TABLESPOONS LEMON JUICE

12 SCALLOPS, ON THE HALF SHELL

PINK SEA SALT (SEE GLOSSARY)

1 SMALL PUNNET CHIVE CRESS OR FINELY
   CHOPPED CHIVES, FOR GARNISHING

EXTRA VIRGIN OLIVE OIL, FOR DRIZZLING

SALT BED

250 G (9 OZ) ROCK SALT

250 G (9 OZ) FINE SEA SALT

12 TAPAS

CEVICHE DE VIEIRA

There's no real structure as to what order we serve dishes at our restaurants except we send out the lightest dishes first and move on to the heavier ones. This is a delicate little dish that we always send out first. Marinated scallops topped with pickled garlic shoots. It's a study in understatement. Enjoy with a chilled glass of albariño.

You will need to begin this recipe the day before.

Thinly slice the garlic shoots into 1 mm (1/32 inch) thick rings. Combine 100 ml (3½ fl oz) of the vinegar, fine salt and sugar in a small non-reactive bowl and stir until dissolved. Add the garlic shoots, cover with plastic wrap and refrigerate overnight.

The next day, combine the remaining vinegar with the lemon juice in a small non-reactive bowl to make a dressing. Set aside.

To make the salt bed, combine the rock and fine salt with 80 ml (2½ fl oz/⅓ cup) of water in a bowl. Place the mixture on a large serving plate or 12 individual plates to make a thick bed for the scallops.

To serve, place the scallops on the salt bed. Sprinkle each with some pink sea salt and spoon on a little of the garlic shoot mixture and 1 teaspoon of the dressing. Garnish with some chive cress and finish with a drizzle of olive oil.

NOTE: Garlic shoots are long green shoots available from Asian grocers and select greengrocers.

MANCHEGO CUSTARD & BLACK TRUFFLE IN AN EGGSHELL

16 TAPAS

CREMA DE QUESO DE MANCHEGO CON HUEVO Y TRUFA

16 EGGS	SEA SALT FLAKES
200 ML (7 FL OZ) MILK	UNCOOKED RICE OR SALT BED (SEE PAGE 105),
400 ML (14 FL OZ) POURING (SINGLE) CREAM	FOR SERVING
100 G (3½ OZ) AGED QUESO DE MANCHEGO	10 G (¼ OZ) FRESH BLACK TRUFFLE
(SEE GLOSSARY), FINELY GRATED	16 PATATAS FRITAS (SEE PAGE 82)
1 SMALL LEEK, WHITE PART ONLY, THINLY	
SLICED	

Chef Robbo (see page 89) of MoVida was excited by a story he read in the paper about a woman who swore by her 'clacker'. It's a device that neatly severs the top off an egg. He was elated because finally he was able to upgrade his signature dish of quail egg with leek purée to a chicken egg filled with Manchego custard. The truffle is a decadence that is perfectly at home here.

Remove the top quarter of each eggshell and discard. If you don't have an egg clacker, use a serrated knife to slowly cut through the shell. Separate the eggs by pouring them into a very clean hand with your fingers slightly apart, and let the eggwhite run between your fingers into a bowl. Place the yolks in another bowl. Keep 4 yolks and use the remaining yolks and eggwhites for another use (see note).

Soak the eggshells in hot water for 20 minutes. Drain and, using your fingernails, very carefully peel away the membrane inside the shell. Rinse the insides carefully with boiling water and leave to drain, cut-side down, on a wire mesh rack.

Preheat the oven to 120°C (235°F/Gas ½). Cover the bottom half of 2 egg cartons with plastic wrap, pushing the plastic into the sockets. Place on a baking tray. Place the eggshells in the cartons (the plastic lining will prevent the eggs from sticking to the carton).

Place the milk, half the cream and the queso de Manchego in a small heavy-based saucepan over high heat. Bring just to the boil, stirring, then reduce the heat to low and simmer for 3 minutes, stirring continuously so the cheese doesn't stick to the base of the pan and a skin doesn't form on the surface. Remove from the heat and allow the flavours to infuse for 5 minutes, stirring occasionally. Strain through a fine sieve to remove any lumps. Lightly whisk the reserved egg yolks. Slowly whisk in the Manchego mixture. Check for seasoning.

Carefully half-fill each eggshell with the Manchego mixture. Bake for 11 minutes, then turn the tray around 180 degrees and continue baking for another 11 minutes. Allow to cool to room temperature. (If you are making these ahead of serving, place the cartons in the fridge until ready to use. Bring to room temperature before serving.

Meanwhile, place the leek and remaining cream in a small saucepan with a pinch of salt over medium heat and cook for 10 minutes or until the leek is tender. Cool slightly, then purée in a food processor. Strain through a fine sieve placed over a bowl, discarding the solids. Cover with plastic wrap and refrigerate for 2 hours or until completely chilled and firm.

To serve, place a mound of rice on a plate and rest an egg on top. Carefully spoon ¼ teaspoon of the leek cream into each egg. Using a Microplane grater, finely grate the truffle onto a plate. Place a generous pinch of truffle into each egg along with a little pinch of salt. Cover each egg with a potato crisp and serve straight away.

NOTE: You can use the egg yolks to make custard or ice-cream. Cover the yolks with plastic wrap and refrigerate for up to 2 days.

PRAWN TERRINE WITH ROMESCO SAUCE

16 TAPAS

GAMBAS CON ROMESCO

500 G (1 LB 2 OZ) PEELED GREEN (RAW) MEDIUM KING PRAWNS (SHRIMP)	**1 BROWN ONION, UNPEELED**
	75 G (2⅔ OZ/½ CUP) HAZELNUTS
5 G (⅛ OZ) MEAT GLUE (SEE GLOSSARY)	**75 G (2⅔ OZ) BLANCHED ALMONDS**
WATERCRESS LEAVES, FOR GARNISHING	**2 TABLESPOONS EXTRA VIRGIN OLIVE OIL, PLUS EXTRA FOR DRIZZLING**
ROMESCO SAUCE	**1 SLICE CRUSTY BREAD, SUCH AS PASTA DURA**
2 RIPE WHOLE TOMATOES	**30 G (1 OZ) SMOKED SWEET PAPRIKA (PIMENTÓN)**
½ GARLIC BULB	
1½ RED CAPSICUM (PEPPERS)	**1 TABLESPOON RED WINE VINEGAR**

This dish is all about the prawn. It's a beautiful block of jellied prawn with a little hit of romesco sauce. The meat glue – an enzyme that reacts with proteins in meat to meld them together – not only sets the prawn meat but also brings the pure prawn flavour to the fore.

Lightly grease and line two 10 cm x 5 cm x 4 cm (4 x 2 x 1½ inch) terrine moulds or loaf (bar) tins with plastic wrap. Finely chop the prawn meat and mix with the meat glue. Fill the tins with the prawn mixture and press down with the back of a spoon. Place each in a high-density plastic bag and follow our steps on sous-vide cooking (see page 123). Vacuum seal the bags, then refrigerate for 1 hour to set.

Meanwhile, make the romesco sauce. Preheat the oven to 180°C (350°F/Gas 4). Place the tomatoes, garlic, capsicum and onion in a roasting tray, drizzle with olive oil and roast for 10 minutes. Remove the tomatoes and set aside. Continue roasting for another 10 minutes, then remove the garlic. Continue roasting for another 20–25 minutes or until the capsicum are slightly charred. Remove the capsicum, place in a bowl and cover with plastic wrap to lightly steam; this will make them easier to peel. Continue roasting the onion for another 15 minutes or until very soft. Remove and set aside.

Spread the nuts on a baking tray and roast for 10–15 minutes or until golden.

When the vegetables are cool enough to handle, peel the tomatoes and discard the skins. Squeeze the garlic cloves from their skins over the tomato. Peel away the skins from the capsicum and discard with the stalks and seeds. Roughly chop the flesh. Remove and discard the outer skin of the onion and roughly chop the flesh.

Heat the olive oil in a heavy-based frying pan over medium heat and cook the bread for about 1½–2 minutes each side or until golden. Drain on paper towel and set aside to cool.

Break the bread into rough pieces and place in a food processor with the nuts and process until coarse breadcrumbs form. Add the paprika, vinegar and roasted vegetables and process until well blended but still coarse in texture. Set aside until ready to use (see note).

Cook the prawn terrines in a water bath at 65°C (149°F) for 20 minutes. Remove the bags from the water bath and refresh in iced water for 15 minutes. Remove the terrines from the bags Turn out the terrines and trim the sides with a sharp knife to make them straight, then cut each into 8 even-sized cubes.

To serve, place the cubes on a serving plate, top each with a small dollop of romesco sauce and garnish with a watercress leaf. Insert a small skewer into each and serve straight away.

NOTE: This romesco sauce recipe makes a little too much for the prawns. Store the leftover sauce in an airtight container for up to 3 days in the fridge. It is excellent served with vegetables or grilled fish.

SMOKED EEL BRANDADE WITH TOCINO CRISPS

	SMOKED EEL BRANDADE	18 TAPAS
40 G (1½ OZ) TOCINO (SEE GLOSSARY) OR PANCETTA, THINLY SLICED	1 X 800 G (1 LB 12 OZ) SMOKED EEL (SEE NOTE)	BRANDADA DE ANGUILA AHUMADA
10 G (¼ OZ) BUTTER	1 TABLESPOON EXTRA VIRGIN OLIVE OIL	
½ BROWN ONION, FINELY DICED	1 BROWN ONION, FINELY DICED	
80 G (2¾ OZ/1 BUNCH) SORREL	2 GARLIC CLOVES, SLICED	
1 TABLESPOON EXTRA VIRGIN OLIVE OIL	2 BAY LEAVES	
TABASCO SAUCE, TO TASTE	4 GUINDILLAS (SEE GLOSSARY), DRAINED AND CHOPPED	
18 FILO CRACKERS (SEE PAGE 98)	200 ML (7 FL OZ) MILK	
BLACK SEA SALT (SEE GLOSSARY)	200 ML (7 FL OZ) POURING (SINGLE) CREAM	
1 TABLESPOON FINELY CHOPPED CHIVES	LEMON JUICE, TO TASTE	
FRESH HORSERADISH ROOT, FOR GARNISHING	SEA SALT FLAKES	

Chef Ewan of MoVida Aqui was playing around with our salt cod brandade recipe one day and he substituted smoked eel for the cod. The resulting mousse had the most sublime silky mouthfeel.

You will need to begin this recipe the day before.

To make the smoked eel brandade, use your fingers to peel the skin from the eel and discard; it will come away easily. Remove the bones. Carefully break up the flesh, checking there are no stray bones. Set aside. You should have about 400 g (14 oz).

Heat the oil in a heavy-based saucepan over medium–low heat. Add the onion, garlic, bay leaves and guindilla and cook for 12 minutes or until the onion is soft and translucent. Add the eel and cook for 10 minutes. The eel will become softer as it cooks. Add the milk and cream and bring to a simmer. Continue to simmer for 12 minutes, stirring occasionally as it thickens. Allow to cool a little, remove the bay leaves, then process in a food processor for 5 minutes or until it is a smooth cream-like consistency. Add the lemon juice. Strain through a fine sieve placed over a bowl, pushing the purée through with the back of a spoon. Allow to cool, then cover with plastic wrap and refrigerate overnight. When cold, season with sea salt.

The next day preheat the oven to 180°C (350°F/Gas 4). Place the tocino on a baking tray lined with baking paper. Cover with more baking paper and place a tray on top. Bake for 12 minutes or until crisp. Cool on the tray.

Melt the butter in a small heavy-based saucepan over low heat. Cook the onion for 8 minutes or until soft. Add the sorrel and cook for 6 minutes or until completely wilted. Transfer to a blender with the oil, a few drops of Tabasco sauce and a pinch of salt and blend for 4 minutes or until smooth. Serve at room temperature.

To serve, using the back of a teaspoon, smear 1 teaspoon of the sorrel sauce over each cracker. Make small quenelles of brandade and place one on each cracker. Insert a tocino crisp into the brandade. Garnish with a sprinkle of black sea salt and chives and finely grate over some horseradish.

CHORIZO-FILLED FRIED POTATO BOMBS WITH SPICY SAUCE

20 TAPAS

BOMBAS CON SALSA BRAVA Y MOJO PICÓN

300 G (10½ OZ) **ROCK SALT**

1 KG (2 LB 4 OZ) **FLOURY POTATOES, SUCH AS RUSSET, UNPEELED**

1¼ TABLESPOONS **EXTRA VIRGIN OLIVE OIL**

SEA SALT FLAKES

200 G (7 OZ/1⅓ CUPS) **PLAIN (ALL-PURPOSE) FLOUR**

4 EGGS, **LIGHTLY BEATEN**

200 G (7 OZ) **PANKO (JAPANESE) BREADCRUMBS (SEE NOTE)**

SUNFLOWER OR OLIVE OIL, FOR DEEP-FRYING

CHORIZO FILLING

2 TEASPOONS **EXTRA VIRGIN OLIVE OIL**

1 SMALL **BROWN ONION, FINELY DICED**

250 G (9 OZ) **FRESH CHORIZO (SEE GLOSSARY)**

150 ML (5 FL OZ) **FINO SHERRY (SEE GLOSSARY)**

½ TEASPOON **SMOKED SWEET PAPRIKA (PIMENTÓN)**

1 SMALL PINCH **SMOKED HOT PAPRIKA**

MOJO PICÓN

2½ TABLESPOONS **CUMIN SEEDS**

2½ TABLESPOONS **FENNEL SEEDS**

1½ **RED CAPSICUM (PEPPER)**

225 ML (7⅔ FL OZ) **EXTRA VIRGIN OLIVE OIL, PLUS EXTRA FOR DRIZZLING**

FINE SEA SALT

1½ TABLESPOONS **SMOKED SWEET PAPRIKA**

½ TEASPOON **SMOKED HOT PAPRIKA**

100 ML (3½ FL OZ) **SHERRY VINEGAR**

1 **GARLIC CLOVE**

SALSA BRAVA

200 G (7 OZ) **ALIOLI (SEE PAGE 54)**

75 ML (2⅓ FL OZ) **TOMATO KETCHUP**

TABASCO SAUCE, TO TASTE

1½ TABLESPOONS **LEMON JUICE**

Despite having several components, this is quite an easy dish to make. In Barcelona, where this dish was invented, it is served only with alioli and a red pepper sauce. Here we break the rules and serve it with a spicy sauce from the Canary Islands – mojo picón.

Preheat the oven to 180°C (350°F/Gas 4). To make the bombas, spread the rock salt evenly over a baking tray and place the potatoes on top. The salt helps to draw out any excess moisture from the potatoes. Bake for 45 minutes or until the potatoes are cooked through.

Meanwhile, make the chorizo filling. Heat the oil in a large saucepan over medium heat and sauté the onion for 6–8 minutes or until soft and translucent. Peel the skin from the chorizo and discard. Crumble the meat into the pan. Sauté for 10 minutes. Add the sherry and simmer for 1 minute. Add the sweet and hot paprika and continue simmering until the sherry has evaporated. Check the seasoning. Allow to cool slightly, then transfer to a food processor and process to a coarse paste. Cool, cover and refrigerate until ready to use.

When the potatoes are cooked, allow to cool just enough to handle, then peel. Mash the flesh with the olive oil until smooth. Season to taste. Take 1 heaped tablespoon (about 45 g/1⅔ oz) and roll into a ball in your hands. Poke your index finger halfway through the ball to make a hole. Fill the hole with about ½ teaspoon of the chorizo filling. Close the hole, roll into a smooth ball and place on a tray. Continue the process until you have used up the mashed potato and filling. Cover the bombas with plastic wrap and refrigerate for 1 hour or until firm.

Meanwhile, make the mojo picón. Spread the spices on a roasting tray lined with baking paper and roast for 5 minutes at 180°C. Allow to cool, then grind in a spice grinder or in a mortar and pestle until a fine powder. Pass through a fine sieve and set aside.

Remove the baking paper from the tray. Place the capsicum on the tray, drizzle with the extra oil and sprinkle with salt. Roast for 35–45 minutes or until the capsicum are blackened and blistered. Place in a bowl and cover with plastic wrap to lightly steam; this will make them easier to peel. When the capsicum are cool enough to handle, peel away the skins and discard with the stalks and seeds. Reserve any juices. Roughly chop the flesh and place in a food processor with 1 tablespoon of the ground spices, both paprikas, olive oil, vinegar, garlic and about 1 tablespoon of the reserved juices and process for 2 minutes or until smooth. Set aside (see notes).

To make the salsa brava, place all of the ingredients in a small bowl and mix well. Set aside (see notes).

To crumb the bombas, arrange 3 plates with a lip or wide shallow bowls in a row. Place the flour in the first, the beaten egg in the second and the breadcrumbs in the third. Roll the bombas in the flour, dip in the egg, allowing the excess to drain off, then roll in the breadcrumbs, coating well, and place on a tray.

Fill a large heavy-based saucepan or deep-fryer one-third full with oil and heat to 170°C (325°F) or until when a cube of bread dropped into the oil takes 20 seconds to turn golden. Deep-fry the bombas, in batches, for 3–4 minutes or until golden all over and hot on the inside. Drain on paper towel.

To serve, spoon small dollops of salsa brava onto a serving plate, then place a bomba on top of each; the sauce will stop the bomba from slipping around. Garnish each with a dollop of the mojo picón and salsa brava and serve straight away.

NOTES: The mojo picón recipe makes more than you will need. Store leftover sauce in an airtight container for up to 1 week in the fridge.

The salsa brava also makes more than you need. Store leftover sauce in an airtight container for up to 3 days in the fridge.

PORK-STUFFED CALAMARI WITH SQUID INK DRESSING

SERVES 4-6

CALAMARES RELLENOS

12 SMALL (ABOUT 8 CM/3¼ INCHES LONG)
  WHOLE CALAMARI

OLIVE OIL, FOR DEEP-FRYING

PORK FILLING

60 ML (2 FL OZ/¼ CUP) EXTRA VIRGIN OLIVE OIL

1 KG (2 LB 4 OZ) PIG CHEEKS, SKIN ON

SEA SALT AND FRESHLY GROUND BLACK
  PEPPER

1 X 200 G (7 OZ) PIG TROTTER

1 BROWN ONION, FINELY DICED

2 GARLIC CLOVES, CHOPPED

1 BAY LEAF

200 ML (7 FL OZ) FINO SHERRY
  (SEE GLOSSARY)

3 LITRES (105 FL OZ) CHICKEN STOCK

SMALL HANDFUL PARSLEY LEAVES,
  FINELY CHOPPED

SQUID INK DRESSING

1½ TABLESPOONS EXTRA VIRGIN OLIVE OIL

½ BROWN ONION, FINELY DICED

100 ML (3¼ FL OZ) FINO SHERRY

1 BAY LEAF

1 TABLESPOON SQUID INK (SEE NOTE)

TO SERVE

1 LEMON, HALVED

PARSLEY CRESS OR FINELY CHOPPED
  PARSLEY LEAVES, FOR GARNISHING

EXTRA VIRGIN OLIVE OIL, FOR DRIZZLING

PINK SEA SALT (SEE GLOSSARY),
  FOR GARNISHING

"You never see pigs and calamari swimming side by side," remarked Chef Robbo (see page 88) of MoVida one day, "but it seems they were meant for each other. Together they taste so good." This is a beautiful dish, a classic Spanish combination.

To make the pork filling, heat the olive oil in a large heavy-based frying pan over medium–high heat. Cook the pig cheeks for 5 minutes each side or until browned. Season with salt while cooking. Remove from the pan and set aside. Cook the pig trotter for 8 minutes or until the skin starts to just brown a little. Remove from the pan and set aside with the cheeks.

Reduce the heat to medium. Add the onion, garlic and bay leaf and cook, stirring occasionally, for 5 minutes or until the onion is soft and translucent. Add the cheeks and trotter, sherry and stock. Increase the heat to high, bring to the boil and skim off any impurities that rise to the surface. Reduce the heat to medium–low and simmer gently for 2½ hours or until the meat is very tender and starting to fall apart. Remove the cheeks and trotter from the pan and set aside to cool. Increase the heat to medium and continue cooking the liquid for 10 minutes or until reduced by half.

When the meat is cool enough to handle, remove and discard the skin from the cheeks. Finely chop the cheek meat and place in a bowl. Remove the meat, skin and half of the fat from the trotter. Finely chop the trotter meat and place in the bowl. Add 250 ml (9 fl oz/1 cup) of the reduced cooking liquid and the parsley. Check the seasoning, mix well and set aside.

To clean the calamari, take a hold of its tentacles and pull them out of the hood. Discard the tentacles. Remove the clear quill from the hoods and scrape away any remaining innards. Leave the skin on the hoods and rinse. Pat very dry, inside and out, with a clean tea (dish) towel.

Fill a large heavy-based saucepan or deep-fryer one-third full with olive oil and heat to 170°C (325°F) or until a cube of bread dropped into the oil takes 20 seconds to turn golden. Dip the calamari in the oil, one at a time, for 5 seconds to seal the meat. Drain on a plate lined with a tea towel.

Trim each calamari hood at both ends to create a 5 cm (2 inch) long tube. If there are wings attached, trim them so they sit flush with the tube. Spoon the pork mixture into each tube and place on a tray lined with baking paper. Refrigerate until ready to use.

Preheat the oven to 250°C (500°F/Gas 9). Place the stuffed calamari on a baking tray lined with baking paper and bake for 8 minutes or until hot inside.

Meanwhile, make the squid ink dressing, heat the olive oil in a saucepan over medium–low heat and cook the onion for 10 minutes or until soft and translucent. Add the sherry and bay leaf and simmer for 8–10 minutes or until reduced by half. Add the squid ink and cook for 3 minutes. Remove the bay leaf and transfer the mixture to a blender. Purée for 2 minutes or until smooth. Check the seasoning. Set aside.

To serve, place the stuffed calamari on a warmed serving plate, squeeze over a little lemon juice and dress the plate with a little squid ink dressing. Top with a scant amount of parsley cress, drizzle over the oil and sprinkle with the pink sea salt.

NOTE: Squid ink is available from select fishmongers and gourmet food stores.

SOUS-VIDE COOKING

Sous vide is a French term meaning under vacuum. It's a cooking technique developed about 35 years ago that involves placing food, generally protein, in a high-density plastic bag, then all the air in the bag is sucked out to create a vacuum. The bag is then lowered into water that is heated to a certain temperature ranging from just above blood temperature to generally about 85°C (185°F). These low temperatures and often long cooking times mean food such as red meat remains tender and juicy; red meat cooked sous vide slices like butter cut with a hot knife. Sous-vide cooking can also set the meat on a chicken leg without it losing a drop of juice. Like many modern chefs we see it as just another tool or technique to let the product speak for itself. This is at the heart of our style of modern Spanish cooking.

---- The full sous-vide gear for a commercial kitchen costs about as much as a great TV and sound system. It's not the sort of stuff most home cooks would consider investing in. But it hasn't stopped some – there are domestic solutions to sous-vide cooking available online that are affordable for the enthusiastic foodie. These consist of vacuum sealers and small temperature-control kits that connect up to rice cookers. The results are reliably good.

---- There is a third road that can be followed. It's a little unreliable but fun to play with all the same. It involves using high-density plastic sous-vide bags, which are available online and at specialty food stores. Zip-lock plastic bags can be used but have a 30 per cent failure rate at longer and higher temperatures. The other equipment you will need is a saucepan to act as a water bath and a cooking thermometer. Follow these steps to vacuum seal and sous-vide cook at home:

---- Place your ingredients in a high-density plastic bag or strong zip-lock plastic bag. Close the opening of the bag three-quarters of the way, leaving a small gap. Lower the bag into a bowl of hot water and the air will be expelled from the bag through the gap. Seal the bag completely. If using a high-density plastic bag, tightly fold over the ends five times and secure with a clothes peg.

---- Place an old plate in the base of a large saucepan. Fill the saucepan with water and place on a heat diffuser over a low heat.

---- Place a thermometer into the water bath and heat the water to the desired temperature. If the temperature rises above the desired temperature, remove the pan from the heat and reduce the heat. This may take a few trials to work out. When the temperature stabilises at the desired temperature, gently place the bag into the water bath and cook for the specified time, checking the temperature regularly and adjusting the heat as necessary. You may need to remove the pan off and on the heat or even have the pan halfway over the heat.

---- Whether you invest in a domestic sous-vide set-up or try the process described above, it's important to be aware that sous-vide cooking temperatures are sometimes below the temperature threshold needed to be reached to knock out any dangerous bugs. This means FOOD MUST BE VERY FRESH and your hands, cooking utensils and surfaces must be SCRUPULOUSLY CLEAN.

CRISP LAMB'S BRAINS WRAPPED IN JAMÓN WITH CAPER MAYONNAISE

12–18 TAPAS

SESOS DE CORDERO

3 LAMB'S BRAINS	SUNFLOWER OIL, FOR DEEP-FRYING
100 ML (3½ FL OZ) FINO SHERRY (SEE GLOSSARY)	FINE SEA SALT (SEE GLOSSARY), FOR GARNISHING
4 SPRIGS THYME	
½ BROWN ONION, FINELY CHOPPED	**CAPER MAYONNAISE**
3 GARLIC CLOVES	½ GARLIC CLOVE
6 BLACK PEPPERCORNS	1 EGG, SEPARATED
1 BAY LEAF	2 TEASPOONS DIJON MUSTARD
1 TEASPOON COOKING SALT	2 TEASPOONS WHITE WINE VINEGAR
6 THIN SLICES JAMÓN SERRANO	2 TABLESPOONS SUNFLOWER OIL
FINELY GRATED ZEST OF ½ LEMON	1½ TABLESPOONS EXTRA VIRGIN OLIVE OIL
2 EGGS	2 TABLESPOONS SALTED CAPERS, RINSED AND CHOPPED
30 G (1 OZ) PLAIN (ALL-PURPOSE) FLOUR	
40 G (1½ OZ/⅔ CUP) PANKO (JAPANESE) BREADCRUMBS (SEE NOTE)	2 TEASPOONS FINELY CHOPPED PARSLEY
	2 TEASPOONS FINELY DICED RED ONION

This is Chef Jimmy's (see page 166) dish, which plays on texture. He has taken a dish normally associated with our older generation and made it young and funky. These are irresistible with their crunchy exterior and flavoursome jamón wrapping paired with the smoothness of the brains, set off with a salty-acidic mayo. Enjoy with a glass of light, spicy garnacha.

Soak the brains in a bowl of salted water in the refrigerator for 2 hours. Drain. Place the brains, sherry, 2 sprigs of thyme, onion, garlic, peppercorns, bay leaf, salt and 1.5 litres (52 fl oz) of cold water in a large heavy-based saucepan. Bring just to the boil over high heat, then remove from the heat straight away and allow the brains to cool in the liquid. Once the water has cooled, remove the brains and discard the liquid. Remove and discard any sinew on the brains. Carefully separate the 2 lobes of each brain, place on a tray, cover with plastic wrap and refrigerate until chilled.

Meanwhile, make the caper mayonnaise. Place the garlic clove on a chopping board. Coarsely chop, then sprinkle with a pinch of salt and crush to a paste using the flat side of a heavy knife. Place a bowl on a folded damp tea (dish) towel. This will stop the bowl from moving around during whisking. Place the egg yolk, mustard and garlic paste in the bowl and gently combine using a balloon whisk. (Reserve the eggwhite to make an eggwash to coat the brains.) While whisking continuously, drizzle with the combined oils, a few drops at a time, into the bowl. Each addition of oil needs to be emulsified into the egg yolk mixture before adding more. Continue whisking and slowly adding the oil until it is all used up. The mayonnaise should become gradually thicker. Whisk in 1 teaspoon of warm water to stop the mayonnaise from splitting. Add the capers, parsley and onion and season with salt. Cover with plastic wrap and refrigerate until ready to use.

To crumb the lamb's brains, place the slices of jamón on a bench and sprinkle with the lemon zest. Pick the leaves off the remaining thyme and sprinkle over the jamón. Place a lobe lengthways at the end of each slice of jamón and roll up.

Lightly beat the eggs with the reserved eggwhite. Arrange 3 shallow bowls in a row. Place the flour in the first, the beaten egg in the second and the breadcrumbs in the third. Roll the lobes in the flour, dip in the egg, allowing the excess to drain off, then roll in the breadcrumbs, coating well. Place on a tray, cover with plastic wrap and refrigerate until ready to cook but no longer than 3 hours.

Preheat the oven to 180°C (350°F/Gas 4). Fill a large heavy-based saucepan or deep-fryer one-third full with oil and heat to 165°C (329°F) or until a cube of bread dropped into the oil takes 30 seconds to turn golden. Deep-fry the lobes, in batches, for 3–4 minutes or until golden all over. Place on a baking tray and bake for 3–4 minutes to ensure they are hot inside.

To serve, spread a thick layer of mayonnaise on a serving plate. Cut each brain into 2 pieces to make 12 portions or cut into 3 pieces to make 18 portions. Place each piece on top of the mayonnaise and sprinkle with a little fine sea salt. Serve straight away.

NOTE: Panko breadcrumbs are available from Asian grocers.

SCALLOPS WITH VEGETABLES

SERVES 6

VIEIRAS Y VEDURAS

375 G (13 OZ) PIMIENTOS DE PIQUILLO (SEE GLOSSARY)	SEA SALT AND FRESHLY GROUND BLACK PEPPER
9 SMALL DUTCH CARROTS	18 SCALLOPS, ROE REMOVED
2 POTATOES, PEELED	60 ML (2 FL OZ/¼ CUP) OLIVE OIL
300 G (10½ OZ) FROZEN PEAS, DEFROSTED	SEA SALT AND FRESHLY GROUND BLACK PEPPER
80 ML (2½ FL OZ/⅓ CUP) EXTRA VIRGIN OLIVE OIL	125 G (4½ OZ/½ CUP) ALIOLI (SEE PAGE 54)

Chef Robbo has respectfully deconstructed the classic Spanish tapa dish, the Russian Salad – potatoes, peas, red pepper and carrot – and given it new meaning. His version is a celebration of the earthiness of the vegetables and their fresh crunch and the different textures that can be achieved from a wonderfully fresh scallop.

Drain the peppers, pat dry with paper towel and place in a dehydrator for 18 hours at 60°C (140°F) or until dried and crisp. Alternatively, place on a baking tray lined with baking paper and dry in a non fan-forced oven at the lowest temperature with the door ajar. The time will vary from oven to oven but it should take about 8 hours or overnight. Remove and store in an airtight container until required.

Preheat the oven to 160°C (315°F/Gas 2–3).

Peel and top and tail the carrots. Cut the potato into 1 cm (½ inch) cubes. Discard the scraps. Bring a large saucepan of salted water to the boil. Blanch the carrots for 2 minutes, remove with a slotted spoon and refresh in cold water, then cut in half crossways. Allow the same pan of water to come back to the boil. Blanch the potato for 2 minutes, then drain and spread out on a tray to cool.

Place the carrot, potato and peas in a bowl, dress with extra virgin olive oil and season to taste with salt.

Heat 1 tablespoon of olive oil in a small heavy-based frying pan over high heat. When the oil is very hot, add 6 scallops and sear for 2 minutes or until the surface is caramelised. Remove the pan from the heat, turn the scallops over and cook the other side for a further 30 seconds. Remove the scallops, season both sides with a little salt and pepper and place on a warmed plate near the stovetop to keep warm. Repeat the process with the remaining olive oil and scallops, cooking 6 at a time.

To serve, place 6 serving plates in the oven to gently warm up. Spoon 2 lines of alioli on each plate. Scatter the carrot, potato and peas evenly over the alioli. Place 3 scallops, caramelised-side up, on each plate and season to taste. Crumble over some pieces of dried piquillo pepper and serve immediately.

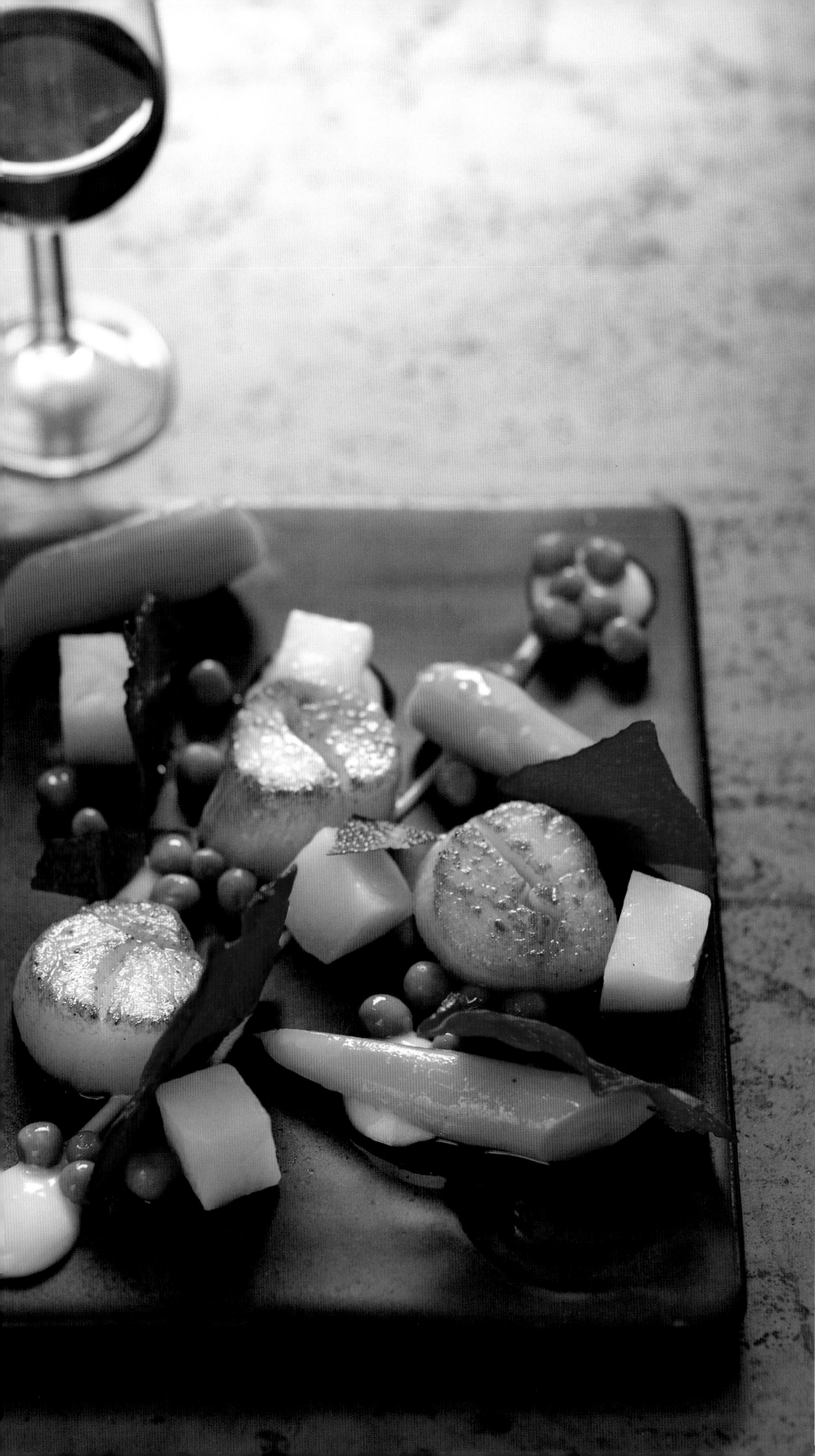

PIQUILLO PEPPERS WITH DEEP-FRIED SALT COD

6 TAPAS

PIMIENTOS
DE PIQUILLO
RELLONOS
DE BACALAO

1 X 400 G (14 OZ) PIECE OF DESALINATED
  REHYDRATED BACALAO FILLET (SEE GLOSSARY)
¼ CUP PARSLEY LEAVES, FINELY CHOPPED
2½ TABLESPOONS LEMON JUICE
2 TABLESPOONS PLAIN (ALL-PURPOSE) FLOUR
OLIVE OR SUNFLOWER OIL, FOR DEEP-FRYING

LEMON DRESSING

1 LEMON
100 ML (3½ FL OZ) CHARDONNAY VINEGAR
100 G (3½ OZ) CASTER (SUPERFINE) SUGAR

SAFFRON BATTER

1 TABLESPOON CASTER (SUPERFINE) SUGAR
15 G (½ OZ) FRESH YEAST (SEE GLOSSARY)

250 G (9 OZ/1⅔ CUPS) PLAIN (ALL-PURPOSE)
  FLOUR
PINCH OF GROUND SAFFRON
1 TABLESPOON FINE SEA SALT

PARSLEY & CAPER SAUCE

50 G (1¾ OZ) CURLY PARSLEY LEAVES
2 TABLESPOONS SALTED CAPERS, RINSED

TO SERVE

6 PIMIENTOS DE PIQUILLO (SEE GLOSSARY),
  DRAINED
BLACK SEA SALT (SEE GLOSSARY),
  FOR GARNISHING

We spent months in the test kitchen developing new dishes for MoVida Aqui and this is one of them. The inspiration came from Casa Labra in Madrid. It's a bar that serves beer, vermouth and juicy morsels of deep-fried salt cod, eaten with your fingers. Our elaboration makes it a more colourful dish.

You will need to begin this recipe the day before.

To make the lemon dressing, thinly slice the lemon and place in a non-reactive bowl. Place the vinegar, sugar and 100 ml (3½ fl oz) of water in a saucepan over high heat and bring to the boil, stirring to dissolve the sugar. Pour over the lemon and allow to cool. Cover and refrigerate overnight.

The next day, make the saffron batter. Place the sugar and 325 ml (11 fl oz) of lukewarm water in a small bowl. Crumble in the yeast and mash together with a fork until the yeast has dissolved completely. Set aside for 15 minutes or until the mixture is foamy. Sift the flour, saffron and salt into a large bowl. Slowly whisk in the yeast mixture, making sure no lumps form. Cover and set aside in a warm place for 30 minutes or until doubled in size.

Meanwhile, make the parsley and caper sauce. Bring a small saucepan of lightly salted water to the boil. Blanch the parsley for a few seconds, drain and refresh under cold running water. Place in a clean tea (dish) towel and wring out the excess water. In a mortar and pestle, add the parsley, capers and 2½ tablespoons of iced water and pound for a few minutes or until smooth. Alternatively, purée in a blender. Set aside.

Cut the bacalao into 6 roughly even-sized baton-shaped portions and place in a large bowl. Add the parsley and lemon juice and season with a pinch of salt. Turn the bacalao in the mixture to coat well. Sprinkle the flour over the bacalao to coat evenly.

Fill a large heavy-based saucepan or deep-fryer one-third full with oil and heat to 180°C (350°F) or until a cube of bread dropped into the oil takes 15 seconds to turn golden. Dip the bacalao in the batter, shaking off any excess, and carefully place in the oil, cooking 2–3 pieces at a time. Deep-fry for 4 minutes or until golden and crisp. Drain on paper towel.

To serve, combine equal parts of the lemon dressing and parsley and caper sauce and drizzle over individual serving plates. Insert a piece of bacalao into a piquillo pepper and place onto the plates. Sprinkle with some black sea salt and serve straight away.

SEA URCHIN WITH FRESH CURD

8 TAPAS

ERIZO DE MAR CON MATO

8 SEA URCHINS, IN THE SHELL (SEE NOTES)	6 SORREL LEAVES (SEE NOTES)
8 SLICES SOURDOUGH BREAD	2 LEMONS, CUT INTO WEDGES
EXTRA VIRGIN OLIVE OIL, FOR DRIZZLING	
SEA SALT FLAKES	**CURD**
6 PIMIENTOS DE PIQUILLO (SEE GLOSSARY),	1 LITRE (35 FL OZ/4 CUPS) MILK
DRAINED	1 ML (1/32 FL OZ) RENNET (SEE GLOSSARY)

The simplest — and best — way to eat sea urchin is to serve its roe on warm toast and butter. This is a polished up version. The rich, creamy texture and heady, salty flavours of the sea urchin work brilliantly with the crunch of the toast and the smoothness of the curd.

Don't be afraid when it comes to cleaning the sea urchins. Hold a sea urchin in one hand, covered with a folded tea (dish) towel. Turn the mouth, which looks like a tiny beak on the small circular area on the spike-free underside, towards you. Pierce the mouth with a pair of sharp kitchen scissors, then cut a 4 cm (1½ inch) circle around the mouth and remove the disc of shell. Discard the disc and gently tap out the loose gravel-like insides and discard. The valuable orange roe is attached to the shell at each end. Using the handle of a teaspoon, gently scoop under one end to detach the roe, then lift out. Carefully pick any pieces of shell or grit from the roe but do not rinse. Set aside. Thoroughly rinse the interior of the shell under running water to clean. Pat dry and place the shells on individual serving plates. Repeat with the remaining sea urchins.

To make the curd, heat the milk in a small saucepan over very low heat to 38°C (100°F). Use a digital thermometer with a probe to ensure the temperature is spot on or the curds will not form properly. Remove from the heat and add the rennet. After 8 minutes the whey should have separated and delicate white curds should have formed. Gently spoon the curd into a fine sieve placed over a bowl (see notes) to drain, then use immediately.

Preheat the oven to 180°C (350°F/Gas 4). Drizzle each slice of bread with a little oil and place on a baking tray. Bake for 5–10 minutes or until golden. Sprinkle with salt.

Cut the pimientos into 5 mm (¼ inch) thick strips. Very thinly slice the sorrel.

To serve, spread 2 teaspoons of the warm curd over each slice of bread, then top with alternate strips of pepper and sea urchin. Squeeze over a little lemon juice and sprinkle with salt. Scatter over some sliced sorrel and drizzle with oil. Place on top of the sea urchin shells and serve straight away.

NOTES: Sea urchins are more readily available and at their best during the winter months. You can buy them from select fishmongers but you may need to order them in advance.

You will only need 2 tablespoons of curd for this dish, although the recipe makes about 300 g (10½ oz). We've found it impractical to make less than this amount. Refrigerate leftover curd in a sieve for 1 hour to drain off any excess liquid, then store in an airtight container in the fridge. Serve with stewed fruit and honey for breakfast or dessert, use in the warm beetroot and shallot salad with fresh curd (see page 76) or grilled sardines (see page 140).

Sorrel is available from select greengrocers.

At the heart of MoVida Aqui is a bed of hot coals — great chunks of charcoal made from native hardwood that burn hot and slow. Throughout service, it pumps out a steady powerful heat. The boys who work the charcoal grill say it's ready to go when the plastic buttons on their chef whites start to melt. The char-grill bars heating above the coals brand the meat the moment it hits the steel. The juices drip down, vaporise and envelop the meat in its own meaty aroma. It's a primal way of cooking. Fearsomely hot and ever changing. Something that needs to be watched, fed, prodded, raked and tended. It's a part of the kitchen that almost seems like it has a life of its own. But then she settles into a steady pulse of heat, ready to meet the orders as they stream in during service. With a good bed of coals and good meat, game, poultry or fish, you don't need to do too much. Let the meat do the talking.

A LA PARRILLA

THE GRILL

GRILLED SARDINES

SARDINILLAS A LA PARRILLA

6 EGGS	EXTRA VIRGIN OLIVE OIL, FOR DRIZZLING
3 X 120 G (4¼ OZ) CANS SARDINILLAS	1 BUNCH CHIVES, FINELY CHOPPED
(SEE GLOSSARY)	
SEA SALT FLAKES	**CURD**
BLACK SEA SALT (SEE GLOSSARY),	2 LITRES (70 FL OZ) MILK
FOR GARNISHING	2 ML (¹⁄₁₆ FL OZ) RENNET (SEE GLOSSARY)

Chef James of MoVida Aqui wanted to create a dish that played on textures and subtle flavours. With the charcoal grill he got his chance. The oils in the sardines are warmed by the heat of the grill and the thin skin is given a crust of bitterness by the charcoal that is smoothed out by the fresh curd and slow-cooked egg. The idea for this dish's presentation is straight from the bars in the south of Spain where they serve food on a sheet of deli paper at the bar.

To cook the eggs, fill a saucepan with water and place on a heat diffuser over low heat. Heat to 65°C (149°F). Check the temperature with a digital thermometer. If it rises above 65°C move the pan off the heat a little until it stabilises at 65°C. Cook the eggs in the water bath for 75 minutes. Remove from the pan.

Meanwhile, drain the sardines and place on a plate lined with paper towel to absorb any excess liquid. Cut out 12 x 20 cm (8 inch) squares of baking paper. Place 2 squares each onto 6 individual serving plates.

Remove the top quarter of each eggshell with an egg clacker (see page 110) and discard. If you don't have an egg clacker, use a serrated knife to slowly cut through the shell. Place the eggs in an egg carton until ready to serve.

To make the curd, heat the milk in a small saucepan over very low heat to 38°C (100°F). Use a digital thermometer with a probe to ensure the temperature is spot on or the curds will not form properly. Remove from the heat and add the rennet. After 8 minutes the whey should have separated and delicate white curds should have formed. Gently spoon the curd into a fine sieve placed over a bowl to drain, then use immediately. Gently crumble 100 g (3½ oz) of the warm curd in the centre of each square of paper.

Meanwhile, heat a barbecue char-grill plate or char-grill pan to high. Place the sardines on a wire mesh tray and char-grill for about 2 minutes each side. Season with salt.

To serve, gently slide a cooked egg out of its shell and onto each plate of curd. Arrange 5 sardines artfully over the curd. Season with a generous pinch of black sea salt, drizzle with olive oil and garnish with the chives.

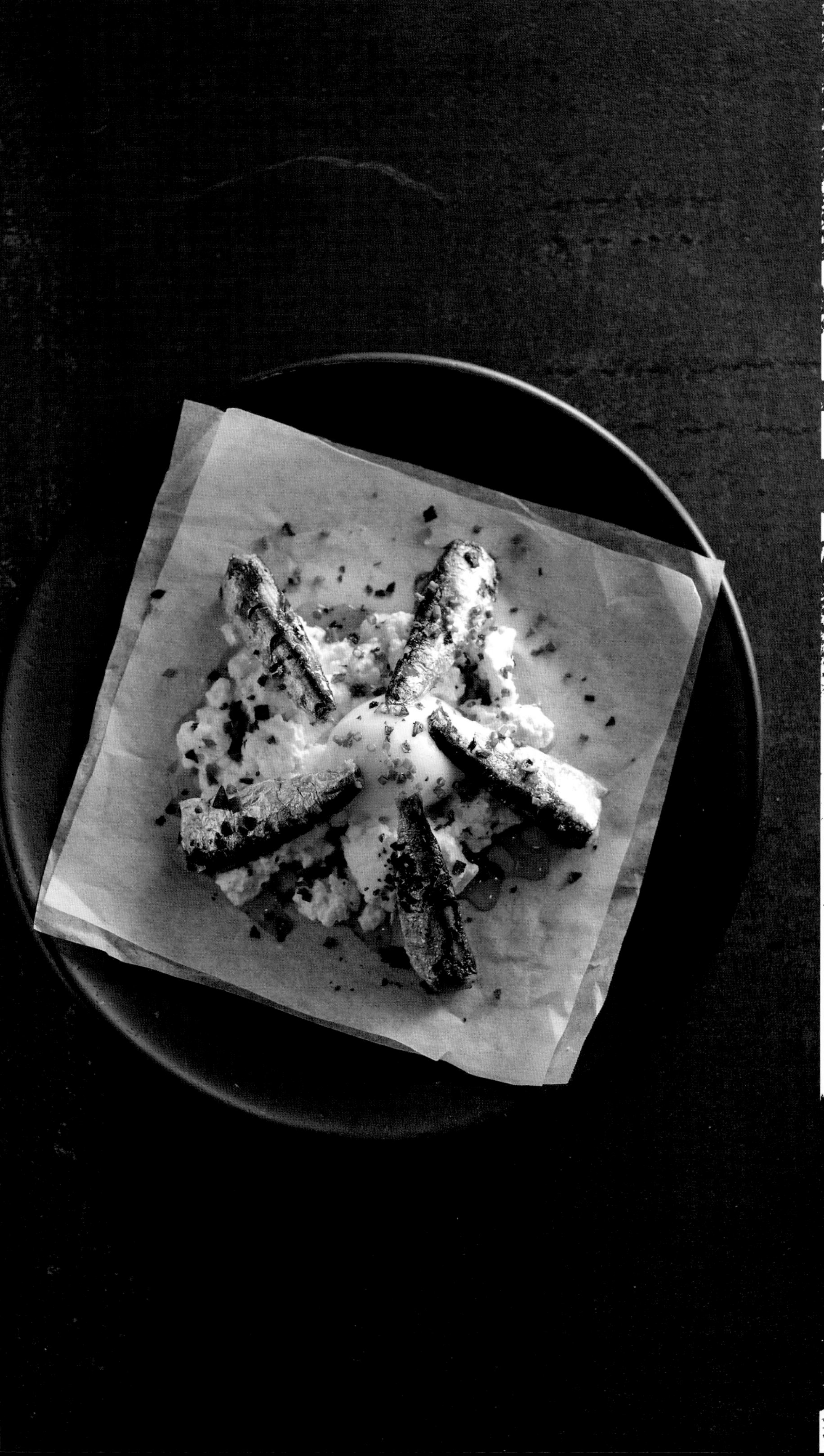

CHAR-GRILLED SQUAB

2 X 500 G (1 LB 2 OZ) SQUABS (PIGEONS)

4 JUNIPER BERRIES

4 BAY LEAVES

2 TABLESPOONS EXTRA VIRGIN OLIVE OIL, PLUS EXTRA FOR DRIZZLING

SEA SALT FLAKES

BLACK SEA SALT, FOR GARNISHING

SERVES 4

PICHÓN A LA PARRILLA

What I love about this dish, apart from the crisp skin, smoky aroma and succulent flesh, is the fact that we use ancient and modern technology to cook it – charcoal and sous vide – side by side. And when it tastes this good, why not? It's best eaten with your fingers.

You will need to remove the legs and breast fillets from each squab. You can discard the remaining wings and carcasses or reserve for making stock. Working with one squab at a time, place the bird, breast-side up, on a chopping board. To remove the legs, spread them to find where the thigh meets the body. At this point, cut through the meat and sinew with a very sharp knife to expose the joint. Push the leg back to pop the bone out of the socket and continue cutting down through the rest of the flesh and skin to remove the leg from the body. Repeat with the other leg. Cut off the tip of the drumstick for a neat presentation.

To remove the wings, cut through the flesh where the wing meets the breast. When you hit the joint, push the wing back and cut through the sinew, then pop the bone out of the socket. Continue cutting through the remaining flesh and skin to remove the wing. Repeat with the other wing.

To remove the breast fillets, slice down between the breastbone and the meat on one side of the squab, following the curve of the ribcage and wishbone with the blade of the knife until the meat is removed from the bones. Repeat on the opposite side. Repeat with the remaining squabs.

Place the legs into a high-density plastic bag with 2 juniper berries, 2 bay leaves and 1 tablespoon of the olive oil. Place the breast fillets in a separate high-density plastic bag with the remaining juniper berries, bay leaves and oil. Follow our steps on sous-vide cooking (see page 123). Vacuum seal the bags and cook the legs in a water bath at 64°C (147°F) for 1½ hours. Cook the breasts in a separate water bath at 60°C (140°F) for 34 minutes. Remove the bags from the water baths and place in iced water to cool down. Remove from the water. (Store for up to 2 days in the fridge.)

Heat a barbecue char-grill plate or char-grill pan to high. Remove the legs and breast fillets from their bags. Char-grill for 2–3 minutes each side or until nice grill marks form and the meat is heated through. Season with salt while cooking.

To serve, garnish with black sea salt, drizzle with oil and serve straight away.

The recipes in this chapter are easy to replicate at home. Buy a bag of charcoal, real charcoal, from a hardware store or wood merchant – a 10-litre (350 fl oz) bucket filled with charcoal will be enough to cook the small amounts of meat in these recipes. Pour the charcoal into a fireproof container, barbecue or even dig a hole in the ground. Spread the charcoal out to make an even bed. Take the largest chunks of charcoal and set them alight over a gas flame. If you don't have a gas stovetop, then use firelighters, but remove the firelighters once the chunks are alight as they can impart a petrol smell to the food. Place the burning pieces onto the bed of charcoal and cover with smaller pieces. Fan the charcoal to establish some flames. You should have a nice little fire by now. Allow it to burn for 15–30 minutes. By this time the fire should be glowing with coals, not leaping with flames. Spread the coals out to form an even bed of glowing embers. Perch a char-grill plate or barbecue mesh (a heavy-duty cake rack will do, too) over the coals at an appropriate distance so that the powerful heat will cook but not burn any meat placed on top. As the heat dies, the grill can be lowered closer to the embers. Every chef knows their grill like the back of their hairless hands and it takes time working a grill to understand its hot spots (generally in the middle) and the cooler spots (generally the corners).

CHAR-GRILLED PIG'S CHEEK WITH RHUBARB BREADCRUMBS

SERVES 10-12

CARRILLDA DE CERDO

6 X 250 G (9 OZ) PIG CHEEKS

1 STAR ANISE

4 BAY LEAVES

250 ML (9 FL OZ/1 CUP) MUSCAT WINE

1 TABLESPOON EXTRA VIRGIN OLIVE OIL, PLUS EXTRA FOR DRIZZLING

SEA SALT AND FRESHLY GROUND BLACK PEPPER

RHUBARB BREADCRUMBS

1 X 2-DAY-OLD LOAF OF BREAD, SUCH AS HIGH TIN OR PASTA DURA, CRUSTS REMOVED

6 STALKS RHUBARB, LEAVES REMOVED

1 TABLESPOON CASTER (SUPERFINE) SUGAR

1 TABLESPOON RED WINE VINEGAR

200 ML (7 FL OZ) EXTRA VIRGIN OLIVE OIL

200 ML (7 FL OZ) SUNFLOWER OIL

1 LARGE BROWN ONION, FINELY DICED

9 GARLIC CLOVES

300 G (10½ OZ) FRESH CHORIZO (SEE GLOSSARY), CUT INTO 1 CM (½ INCH) DICE

300 G (10½ OZ) PANCETTA, CUT INTO LARDONS

150 G (5¼ OZ) MORCILLA (SEE GLOSSARY), CUT INTO 1 CM (½ INCH) DICE

⅓ CUP PARSLEY LEAVES, COARSELY CHOPPED

The Spanish are very particular about their migas. Rough torn breadcrumbs, salted and fried, are part of the very fabric of society. The freedom of cooking Spanish food in another country is that we are unshackled from convention. Here Chef James (see page 234) has brought together traditional ingredients — migas, onions, sausages, fruit and grilled pig cheek — and put them on the one plate; unheard of in Spain.

You will need to begin this recipe the day before.

To begin the rhubarb breadcrumbs, roughly tear the bread into uneven crumbs — the largest about 3 cm (1¼ inches) long — and spread out evenly on a tray. Combine 80 ml (2½ fl oz/⅓ cup) of water with a small pinch of salt in a bowl and stir until dissolved. Using your fingers, flick the salted water evenly over the bread, then stir to combine well. Cover and refrigerate overnight.

Meanwhile, rinse the pig cheeks. Cut the skin off and trim the sinew and fat, keeping in mind fat equals flavour, so don't trim too much off. Place the cheeks in 2 large high-density plastic bags and divide the star anise, bay leaves, wine, 1 tablespoon of olive oil and a pinch of salt and pepper between the bags. Follow our steps on sous-vide cooking (see page 123). Vacuum seal the bags and cook in a water bath at 75°C (167°F) for 24 hours. Remove the bag from the water bath and place in iced water to cool down as quickly as possible. Remove from the water. (You can refrigerate the bag for up to 4 days.)

The next day, continue making the rhubarb breadcrumbs. Lightly remove any fibrous bits from the rhubarb stalks with a vegetable peeler. Cut the rhubarb into 8 cm (3¼ inch) batons. Place in a high-density plastic bag with the sugar and vinegar and vacuum seal. Cook in a water bath at 60°C (140°F) for 1 hour.

Remove the bag from the water bath and place in iced water to cool down as quickly as possible. Refrigerate until ready to use.

Heat both the oils in a large heavy-based frying pan over high heat until hot. Shallow-fry the onion, garlic, chorizo and pancetta for 15 minutes, stirring continuously. The onion should caramelise on the edges and the chorizo should be browned and have released its fat. Pour the mixture into a sieve lined with paper towel placed over a heatproof bowl. Transfer the chorizo mixture to a bowl, reserving the strained oil. Cover the bowl to keep warm.

Return the pan to medium–high heat. Add the morcilla and cook, stirring regularly, for 4 minutes. Don't worry if some of the morcilla crumbles or forms a crust – this adds to the textural nature of the dish. Add the morcilla to the chorizo mixture. Cover to keep warm.

Wipe out the pan with paper towel and return to high heat. Heat half of the reserved strained oil until hot, then add the breadcrumbs. They should sizzle but not burn. Keep them moving by stirring or shaking the pan. After a few minutes they will wilt a little as they take up the oil, then they will start to crisp up. Continue cooking, stirring regularly, for 8–9 minutes or until the bread is crisp and deep golden. Add the chorizo and morcilla mixture, mix well and cook for 1 minute. Strain through a sieve lined with paper towel placed over a heatproof bowl. Remove the rhubarb from its bag, gently reheat, then add to the bowl. Add the parsley to the bowl and season with salt. Cover and keep warm.

Heat a barbecue char-grill plate or char-grill pan to high. Remove the pig cheeks from the bag and char-grill, fat-side down, for 2–3 minutes, season and turn over. Cook the other side for 2–3 minutes and season.

To serve, divide the rhubarb breadcrumbs among warmed serving plates. Top each with a pork cheek, sprinkle with a little salt and drizzle with olive oil.

CHAR-GRILLED FLOUNDER WITH CLAMS

60 ML (2 FL OZ/¼ CUP) LEMON JUICE	2 TABLESPOONS EXTRA VIRGIN OLIVE OIL,
3 GARLIC CLOVES	PLUS EXTRA FOR BRUSHING
40 G (1½ OZ) PIECE OF JAMÓN, CUT INTO	125 ML (4 FL OZ/½ CUP) FINO SHERRY
SMALL CHUNKS	(SEE GLOSSARY)
1 TABLESPOON FINE SEA SALT,	1 TOMATO, PEELED, SEEDED (SEE GLOSSARY)
PLUS EXTRA FOR SEASONING	AND DICED
1 X 900 G (2 LB) WHOLE FLOUNDER, CLEANED	¼ CUP PARSLEY LEAVES, FINELY CHOPPED
	12 SURF OR OTHER CLAMS (VONGOLE), RINSED

SERVES 2
PESCADO A LA PARRILLA

This whole fish, grilled in the Basque style, is best eaten with your hands. We want you to feel the sticky texture of the flesh, to pick up the clams and suck out the meaty morsels within. The sweetest meat on the fish is closest to the bone and this is best extracted with the digits. It's a good idea to serve with a finger bowl.

Combine the lemon juice, 2 garlic cloves, jamón and salt with 100 ml (3½ fl oz) of water in a squeeze bottle to make a brine. Shake well, then set aside for 1 hour for the flavours to meld.

Heat a barbecue char-grill plate or char-grill pan to medium. Wash the flounder and pat dry with paper towel. Season the inside of the flounder with salt, brush the skin with the extra olive oil and char-grill, squirting over a little brine every few minutes, for 5 minutes each side or until cooked through. The flesh should be opaque and flaky when tested with a fork. Place on a tray and give it one last squirt of brine. Loosely cover with aluminium foil and let it rest for a few minutes.

Meanwhile, heat the oil in a saucepan over medium heat. Finely chop the remaining garlic clove and cook for 30–60 seconds but do not let it burn. Add the sherry, bring to the boil, then add the tomato and parsley and simmer for 1 minute. Add the clams, cover with a lid and simmer, shaking the saucepan regularly, for 2–3 minutes or until the clams have opened. Check for seasoning.

To serve, place the fish on a warmed serving plate and spoon over the clams and sauce.

CHAR-GRILLED RUMP STEAK

SERVES 4

BISTEC A LA PARRILLA

2 TEASPOONS COOKING SALT	EXTRA VIRGIN OLIVE OIL, FOR RUBBING
350 G (12 OZ) CAULIFLOWER, BROKEN INTO	SEA SALT AND FRESHLY GROUND
2 CM (¾ INCH) FLORETS	BLACK PEPPER
70 G (2½ OZ) ALMONDS, SLIVERED	40 G (1½ OZ) UNSALTED BUTTER
(SEE NOTES)	1 LEMON
400 G (14 OZ) BEEF RUMP CAP (SEE NOTES),	1 TABLESPOON FINELY CHOPPED PARSLEY
AT ROOM TEMPERATURE	ALMOND OIL (SEE NOTES), FOR DRIZZLING

Almonds are texturally awesome in this dish. The just-tender cauliflower, the juiciness of the char-grilled steak and the crunchiness of the toasted nuts are brought together by the butter and the sharp hit of lemon zest.

Bring a saucepan filled with 500 ml (17 fl oz/2 cups) of water and the salt to the boil. Blanch the cauliflower for 2 minutes or until just al dente. Drain and set aside.

Preheat the oven to 180°C (350°F/Gas 4). Place the almonds on a baking tray lined with baking paper and roast for 6–7 minutes or until golden. Set aside.

Heat a barbecue char-grill plate or char-grill pan to high. Rub the beef with a little olive oil and season with salt and pepper. Char-grill the beef for 6 minutes each side for medium-rare. The meat should still yield slightly to the touch. Remove from the heat, cover loosely with aluminium foil and rest for 4 minutes before serving.

Meanwhile, melt the butter in a large frying pan over medium heat, add the cauliflower and cook for 3 minutes or until warmed through. Add the almonds and season with salt and pepper. Finely grate the zest of the lemon directly over the cauliflower. Add the parsley, drizzle over the almond oil and gently toss to combine.

To serve, arrange the cauliflower on individual serving plates. Slice the beef across the grain and lay over the cauliflower. Finish with a sprinkle of salt and a drizzle of almond oil.

NOTES: If you are very patient, you can cut the almonds into slivers by hand, but we use a food processor with a slicing blade attachment.

Rump is made of three muscle groups: tri-tip, rost biff and cap, which is the full-flavoured muscle with a lovely layer of rich fat. You can order beef rump cap from your butcher.

Almond oil is available from good food stores and health food stores.

154

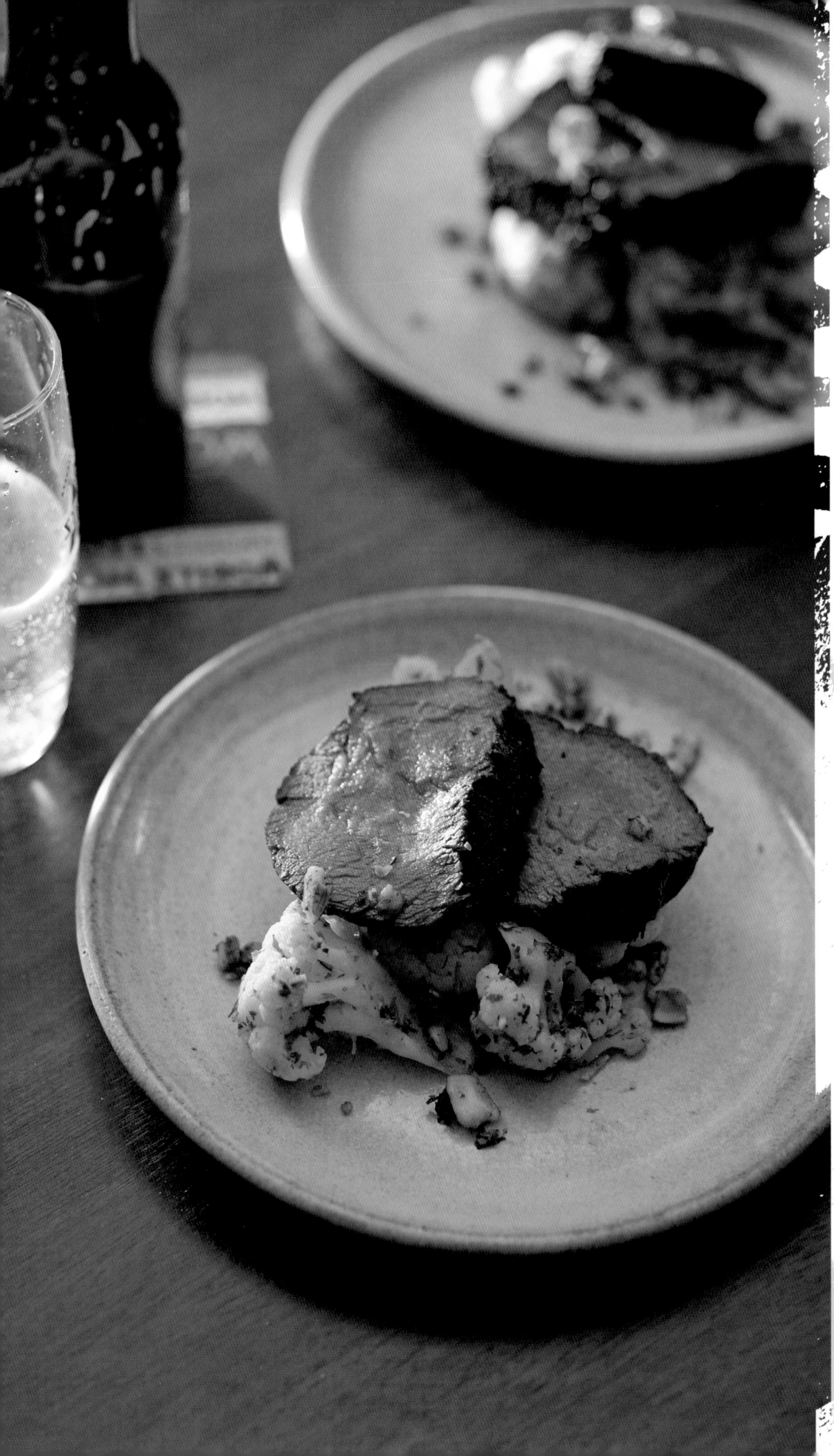

La plancha is the classic Spanish bar cook-top, which can easily squeeze into those tiny spaces in old buildings. Our hotplate is a great big block of solid steel, which we can crank up to 280°C (536°F). It sits right behind the bar. If you order mussels, say, on they go, right in front of you. There's a hiss as they hit the hard steel, the heat dragging the juices out of the flesh and vaporising them. There's a cloud of steam Iceland would be proud of and the aroma of food and its juices being seared by the heat. On go vegetables, mushrooms and seafood: prawns (shrimp), razor clams, crayfish (rock lobsters), scampi (langoustines), fish, squid. Our super-succulent pig's ears and sweetbreads also get a final flash of heat from the hotplate. Whatever we cook on it, the hotplate imparts a flavour that is distinctively Spanish. Distinctively a la plancha.

A LA PLANCHA

THE HOTPLATE

GRILLED CRAYFISH

SERVES 4-6

BOGAVANTE
A LA PLANCHA

4 X 300 G (10½ OZ) LIVE FRESHWATER CRAYFISH (ROCK LOBSTERS) OR MARRON

½ CUP PARSLEY LEAVES

2 GARLIC CLOVES

125 ML (4 FL OZ/½ CUP) EXTRA VIRGIN OLIVE OIL, PLUS EXTRA FOR SERVING

SEA SALT FLAKES

1½ TABLESPOONS FINO SHERRY (SEE GLOSSARY)

3 TEASPOONS LEMON JUICE

This is the perfect way of cooking freshwater crayfish. Put them to sleep. Cut them in half. Sear the flesh. Scorch the shell. Season. Serve.

Place the live crayfish in the freezer for 30 minutes to put them to sleep. Meanwhile, very finely chop the parsley and garlic and combine with the olive oil in a bowl. Set aside.

To kill the crayfish, cut in half lengthways using a sharp, heavy knife. Remove the digestive tracts with a skewer and discard. Use the back of the knife to crack the shells of the claws.

Heat a barbecue hotplate or flat grill plate to high. Drizzle over a little oil and cook the crayfish, cut-side down, for 3 minutes. Turn over, season the flesh with salt and drizzle with the parsley mixture and sherry. Cook for 5 minutes or until the shells have turned red and the flesh is just cooked through.

To serve, drizzle over the lemon juice and a little oil and season with salt.

CHARO'S GRILLED EGGPLANT

1 TABLESPOON CUMIN SEEDS	125 ML (4 FL OZ/½ CUP) EXTRA VIRGIN OLIVE	**SERVES 4**
1 TABLESPOON FENNEL SEEDS	OIL, PLUS EXTRA FOR COOKING	BERENJENAS
1 GARLIC CLOVE	1½ TABLESPOONS SHERRY VINEGAR	ALIÑADAS
2 LEMONS	4 LEBANESE EGGPLANT (AUBERGINES)	
1 CUP PARSLEY LEAVES, FINELY CHOPPED	SEA SALT FLAKES	

Our restaurants have dishes that migrate from the kitchen at home to the kitchen at work. This is one of those dishes. This is something that Mum, her nickname is Charo, used to make and keep in the fridge for us to put on bocadillos. The hotplate with its heat transforms the flavour of eggplant. Also, try grilling zucchini and mushrooms using this method.

Preheat the oven to 180°C (350°F/Gas 4). Spread the spices evenly over a baking tray and roast for 5 minutes or until aromatic. Allow to cool. Finely grind in a mortar and pestle or in a spice grinder. Add the garlic and pound into a smooth paste. Add the finely grated zest of both lemons and the juice of just one. Add the parsley, olive oil and vinegar and stir to combine. Set aside.

Meanwhile, heat a barbecue hotplate or flat grill plate to high. Cut the eggplant lengthways into 2 mm (1/16 inch) thick slices. Drizzle a little oil over the hotplate and cook the eggplant slices for 30–60 seconds each side or until golden.

To serve, arrange in a serving bowl, drizzle over the dressing and sprinkle over a little salt.

HOTPLATE MUSSELS WITH GARLIC & FINO SHERRY

SERVES 4

MEJILLONES

2 KG (4 LB 8 OZ) MUSSELS	2½ TABLESPOONS EXTRA VIRGIN OLIVE OIL
½ CUP PARSLEY LEAVES	100 ML (3½ FL OZ) FINO SHERRY
2 GARLIC CLOVES	(SEE GLOSSARY)
FINELY GRATED ZEST AND JUICE OF 2 LEMONS	SEA SALT FLAKES

We have a great relationship with our fishmonger. He gets us the best mussels and flies them in from Tasmania. Voluminous and super sweet, we steam them in their shells directly on the hotplate. When the shells get super hot, there's an unmistakable aroma of the pier, the rock pool, fishing boats and the fresh salty sea. Enjoy with gusto and a finger bowl to wash your hands.

Scrub and debeard the mussels by grasping the threads emerging from the shell and pulling back hard to the hinge. Discard the beards.

Chop the parsley and garlic together with the lemon zest.

Heat a barbecue hotplate or flat grill plate to high. If there is enough room, place all of the mussels on the hotplate. If the hotplate is too small, cook the mussels in 2 batches so the hotplate is not overcrowded. Drizzle over the olive oil, half of the sherry and half of the parsley mixture. Cover with the barbecue hood or a roasting tray and allow the mussels to steam for about 5 minutes, lifting the hood occasionally to turn the mussels over. Remove the mussels as they open and place in a bowl. If after 5 minutes there are still unopened mussels, prise them open with a knife, smell to check for freshness and, if there are no offensive odours, add them to the other open mussels.

To serve, season with salt and scatter over the remaining sherry and remaining parsley mixture. Drizzle over the lemon juice and stir to combine.

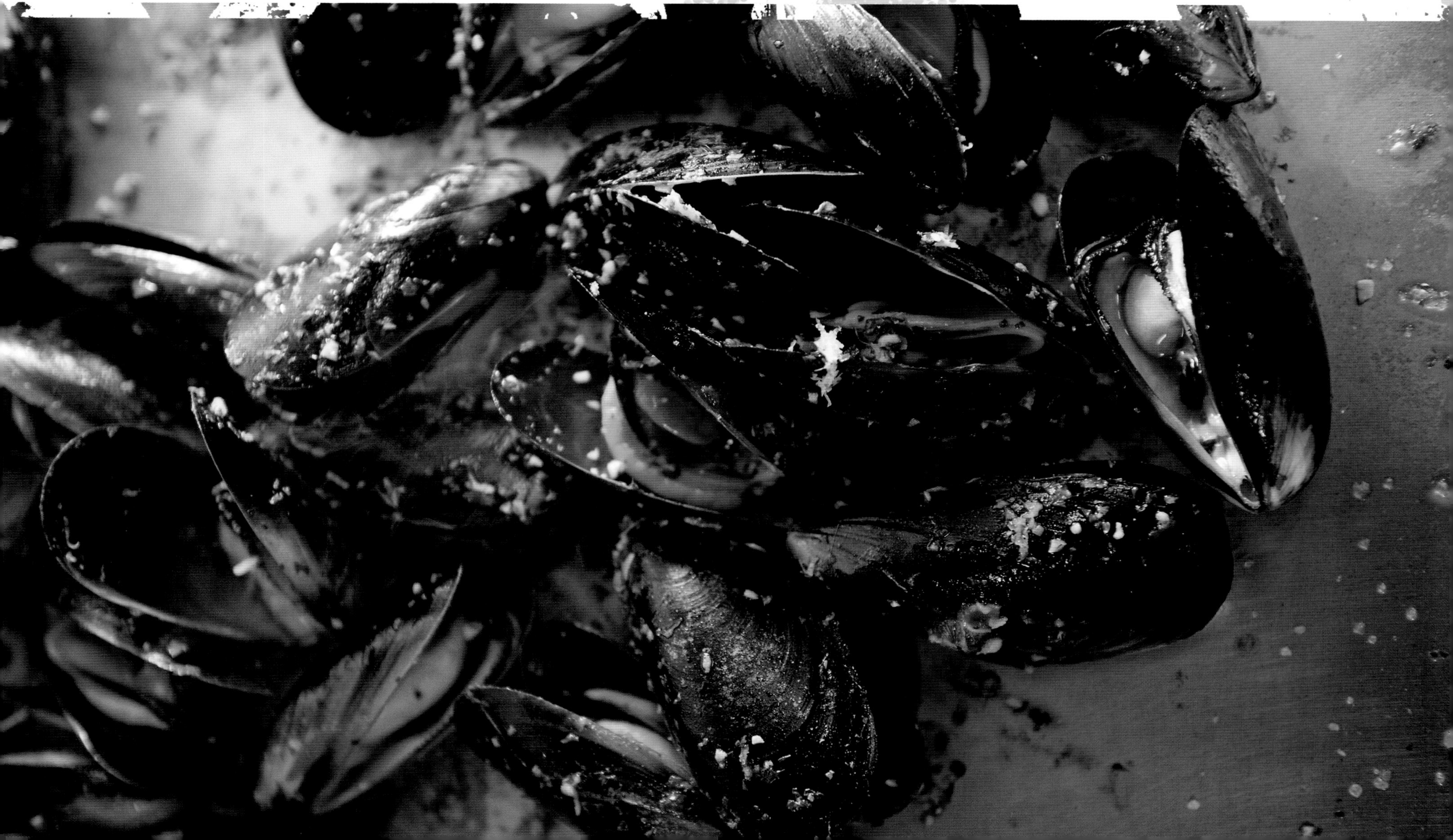

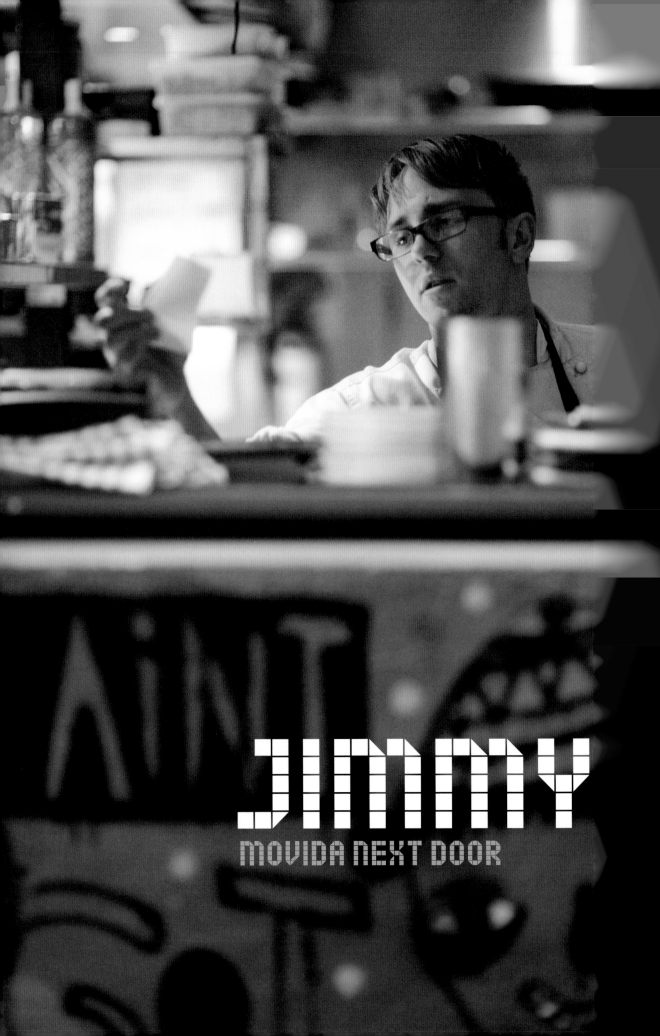

JIMMY
MOVIDA NEXT DOOR

Every night, la plancha at MoVida Next Door gets a pounding. In the bar, fish and shellfish sit splayed on a bed of crushed ice in a glass case. You point to a fish, calamari, marron or cluster of mussels and Chef Jimmy will have it sizzling on la plancha and then on a plate in front of you within minutes. Order a glass of chilled sherry and you could imagine you're on the Atlantic coast of Andalusia. But you're not, you're in Melbourne, in a little bar looking out onto the icons of Melbourne: The MCG; Federation Square and the graffiti of Hosier Lane. This is Chef Jimmy's domain.

---- He's a quietly spoken lad from Tasmania. When he talks it is generally important. He's made his way up the ranks and turns out some really beautiful dishes from his open kitchen. MoVida Next Door has turned out to be our training ground where younger chefs can master a smaller menu, show their talents and learn how to work a team. Like all our chefs, Chef Jimmy has his signature dishes. In them he expresses himself with darker flavours and plays on texture. Sometimes I have to remember he's still in his twenties – an old head on young shoulders.

BLACK-SKINNED FLATHEAD

3 LEBANESE EGGPLANT (AUBERGINES)	1½ TABLESPOONS EXTRA VIRGIN OLIVE OIL, PLUS EXTRA FOR COOKING
120 G (4¼ OZ) HONEY	3 GARLIC CLOVES, SLICED
120 ML (4 FL OZ) SHERRY VINEGAR	550G (1 LB 4 OZ) SURF OR CLAMS (VONGOLE), PURGED
SEA SALT FLAKES	200 ML (7 FL OZ) FINO SHERRY (SEE GLOSSARY)
6 X 200 G (7 OZ) FLATHEAD FILLETS, SKIN ON	½ CUP PARSLEY LEAVES, CHOPPED
165 G (5¾ OZ) BUTTER	
3 BAY LEAVES	

SERVES 6

PESCADO A LA PLANCHA

Flathead is the great Aussie fish. If you're living in a part of the world where you can't get flathead – I'm sorry – use hake or another fine white-fleshed fish. This is another example where old and new cooking techniques marry. The sous-vide cooking sets the protein and flavours every last morsel of flesh, while the quick dance on la plancha gives the fish skin a shiny finish like black glass.

Peel the eggplant with a vegetable peeler or sharp knife and cut each in half crossways. Place each piece in separate high-density plastic bags. Combine the honey and vinegar in a small bowl. Add 2 tablespoons to each bag with a pinch of salt. Follow our steps on sous-vide cooking (see page 123). Vacuum seal the bags and cook in a water bath at 84°C (183°F) for 15 minutes or until soft. Remove the bags from the water bath and set aside to cool. Remove the eggplant from the bags and cut each piece crossways into 4 slices. Set aside.

Run your fingers over the flathead fillets and, using a pair of fish tweezers, remove all the fine pin bones. Dip the tweezers into a small bowl of water to get the bones off. Place 2 fillets each in high-density plastic bags with a pinch of salt, 15 g (½ oz) of the butter and 1 bay leaf. Vacuum seal the bags and cook in a water bath at 55°C (131°F) for 10 minutes. The fish will look opaque and cooked through. Remove the bags from the water bath. Remove the fillets from the bags and set aside.

Heat the olive oil in a large heavy-based saucepan over medium–high heat. Add the garlic and cook for 2 minutes or until just golden. Add the clams and sherry, cover and cook for 5–8 minutes or until all the clams have opened. Add the remaining butter, the parsley and eggplant. Cook, uncovered, for about 3 minutes or until the liquid has reduced by half. Cover to keep warm.

Meanwhile, heat a barbecue hotplate or flat grill plate to high. Drizzle over a little oil and cook the flathead, skin-side down, for 2 minutes, season with salt and remove from the heat.

To serve, place a fillet, skin-side up, on a warmed plate and divide the clam mixture among the plates, spooning over the pan juices. Serve straight away.

GRILLED CUTTLEFISH WITH SQUID INK SAUCE

SERVES 4-6

CHOCOS A LA PLANCHA CON SU TINTA

2 KG (4 LB 8 OZ) SMALL WHOLE CUTTLEFISH

½ CUP PARSLEY LEAVES

2 GARLIC CLOVES

125 ML (4 FL OZ/½ CUP) EXTRA VIRGIN OLIVE OIL, PLUS EXTRA FOR COOKING

SEA SALT FLAKES

100 ML (3½ FL OZ) FINO SHERRY (SEE GLOSSARY)

1½ TABLESPOONS LEMON JUICE

WATERCRESS SPRIGS, FOR GARNISHING

SQUID INK SAUCE

3 BROWN ONIONS, QUARTERED

1 HEAPED TEASPOON SQUID INK (SEE NOTE)

½ TEASPOON SEA SALT FLAKES

500 ML (17 FL OZ/2 CUPS) FINO SHERRY

Cuttlefish and calamari are close companions of la plancha. The heat of the hotplate sucks out some of the juice in the seafood and partially steams the flesh while the surface browns and caramelises, giving both succulence and big flavour.

To make the squid ink sauce, place the onion, squid ink, salt and sherry in a pressure cooker. Secure the lid and follow the manufacturer's instructions to bring to pressure over high heat. Once under pressure, which you'll know as it will be hissing from its valve, reduce the heat to medium and cook under pressure for 30 minutes. Alternatively, place the onion, squid ink, salt and sherry in a saucepan over medium heat. Cover and cook for 1 hour or until the onions are very soft.

Allow to cool slightly, then purée using a stick blender or in a food processor. Set aside.

To clean the cuttlefish, take a hold of its tentacles and pull them out of the hoods. Discard the tentacles. Gently tear off the wings and discard. Remove the clear quills and scrape away any remaining innards. Peel the skin off. Cut the hoods open along what appears to be a seam, then cut into 3cm (1¼ inch) squares. Rinse and drain well.

Finely chop the parsley and garlic and combine with the olive oil in a large bowl. Set aside.

Heat a barbecue hotplate or flat grill plate to high. Drizzle over a little oil and cook the cuttlefish on one side for 2 minutes or until golden. Season with salt, then turn over and cook the other side for 2 minutes. Add the cuttlefish to the parsley mixture. Add the sherry and lemon juice, season with salt and stir to combine.

To serve, spoon the squid ink sauce over warm plates and top with the cuttlefish. Garnish with a few sprigs of watercress and serve straight away.

NOTE: Squid ink is available from select fishmongers and gourmet food stores.

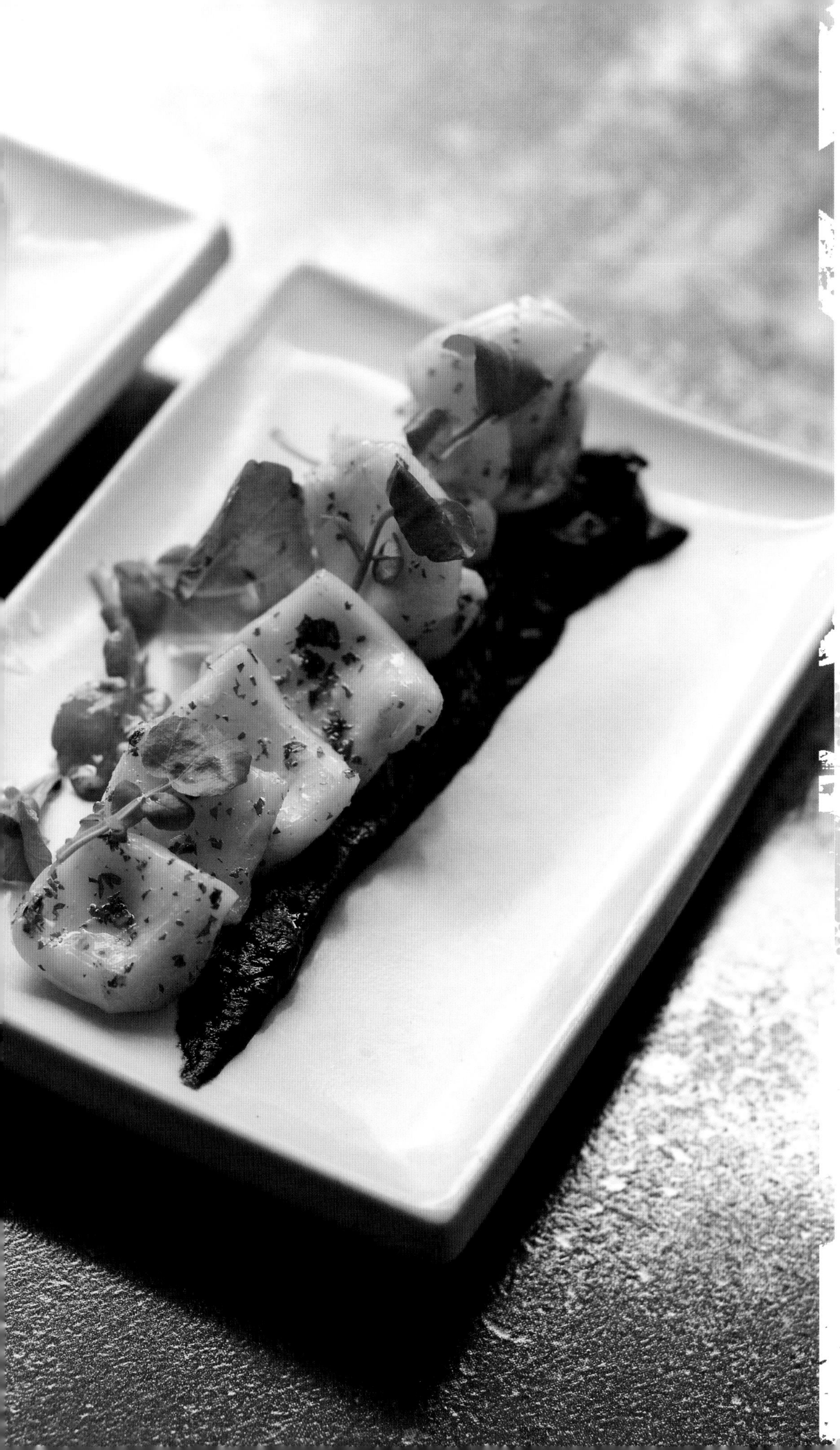

QUAIL WITH TOASTED CORN

SERVES 4

CORDONIZ CON KIKOS

100 G (3½ OZ) KIKOS (TOASTED GIANT CORN KERNELS)

2 LARGE QUAILS

EXTRA VIRGIN OLIVE OIL, FOR DRIZZLING

SEA SALT AND FRESHLY GROUND BLACK PEPPER

BLACK SEA SALT

CHOPPED FLAT-LEAF (ITALIAN) PARSLEY LEAVES, TO GARNISH

PÂTÉ

300 G (10½ OZ) CHICKEN LIVERS, CLEANED

½ SMALL BROWN ONION, THINLY SLICED

1 TEASPOON EXTRA VIRGIN OLIVE OIL

PINCH THYME LEAVES

SEA SALT FLAKES

60 ML (2 FL OZ/¼ CUP) PEDRO XIMÉNEZ SHERRY

60 ML (2 FL OZ/¼ CUP) THICKENED CREAM

40 G (1½ OZ) UNSALTED BUTTER, SOFTENED

CORN PURÉE

5 COBS CORN, HUSKS AND SILKS REMOVED

160 ML (5¼ FL OZ) MILK

80 G (2¾ OZ) BUTTER

There are classics and there is evolution. This little quail dish is one of Chef Robbo's and started as a layer of pâté under the seared bird. Inspired by the flavour-enhancing properties that pâté brings to quail meat, Chef Jimmy tweaked the dish, sliding the pâté under the quail skin and adding a rich purée of corn to finish. The freshest corn will give the best results.

To make the pâté, preheat the oven to 170°C (325°F/Gas 3). Place the livers, onion, olive oil, thyme and a pinch of salt in a small baking dish, mix together well and bake for 20 minutes or until the livers are cooked through but still slightly pink in the middle. Remove from the oven and allow to cool slightly.

Place the cooled liver mixture in a food processor, add the sherry, cream and butter and process for several minutes or until very smooth. Check the seasoning and add salt to taste. Push the mixture through a fine sieve into a small bowl. Cover with plastic wrap and refrigerate until needed.

Meanwhile, make the corn purée. To remove the corn kernels, hold each corn cob by the stalk with the tip of the cob on the bench and run a very sharp knife under the kernels from the base to the tip. Place the kernels, milk and butter in a wide-based saucepan over medium–low heat and cook, stirring occasionally, for 20 minutes or until the corn is tender. Allow to cool a little, then purée in a blender until smooth. Push through a fine sieve into a bowl, cover with plastic wrap and place in the fridge until needed.

Place the kikos in a food processor and process to form coarse crumbs. Set aside.

Meanwhile, to debone the quails, working with one quail at a time, place the bird, breast-side up, on a chopping board. Slice down between the breastbone and breast meat with a sharp knife. Follow the ribcage, then along the wishbone with the blade of the knife. When you come to the wing joint, push the wing back to reveal the joint, cut the connective tissue and pop the bone out of the socket. Continue cutting down until you reach the leg joint. Carefully cut through the tendons, then pop the bone out of the socket and cut along the spine. With a pair of kitchen scissors cut off the wing tip and the tip of the leg bone. Remove the thigh bone by running the tip of the knife along the bone and working the flesh away from the bone. Gently pull the bone from the flesh and discard. Repeat on the other side. You should have 2 halves with breast, boneless leg and wing with one bone in. Repeat with the other quail. Set the quail halves aside and discard the carcasses.

Tuck the leg meat under the breast and use any excess skin to wrap over the leg. Lift the skin away from the breast meat and place a teaspoon of the pâté between the breast and the skin on each quail half. (Store any excess pâté, covered, in the refrigerator for up to 2 days. Serve on pieces of toasted bread as an appetiser.)

Preheat a charcoal or gas barbecue to high. Season the quail with salt and pepper and drizzle with a little olive oil. Grill the quail for 2 minutes on each side, the quail should still be a little pink inside. Allow to rest in a warm place for 5 minutes.

To serve, place 2 tablespoons of corn purée on each plate and top with a piece of quail. Sprinkle over 1 tablespoon of kikos crumbs and finish with a little black sea salt, parsley and olive oil.

There's a bright red bubbling mass of tomato, onion and capsicum slowly cooking down to a deep-red, thick jam-like sofrito. This will become the base for our paellas. The space in the kitchen at our latest addition, MoVida Aqui, gave us the possibility to cook rice dishes properly for the first time. Paellas are big and require space. The bratt pan, an industrial piece of cooking equipment, we use to cook sofrito in is one metre (39½ inches) across. The spoon used for mixing the sofrito looks like one of those joke spoons you see in souvenir shops with the words World's Greatest Stirrer painted on. Every time a chef walks past the sofrito pan, they can't help themselves but give the sofrito a little stir. To feed this hungry beast, there's always someone chopping capsicum, onions and tomatoes. Spanish rice dishes range from wet soupy perols to paellas with socarrat, a beautiful dark crust on the bottom. They can be many things but they need to always be made fresh so the rice still has some bite and hasn't bloated on the stock in which it was cooked.

ARROCES
RICE

EASY RICE

SERVES 6

ARROZ
SENCILLO

1 X 600 G (1 LB 5 OZ) WHOLE CALAMARI

500 G (1 LB 2 OZ) MUSSELS

60 ML (2 FL OZ/¼ CUP) EXTRA VIRGIN OLIVE OIL

SEA SALT FLAKES

1 BROWN ONION, FINELY DICED

2 GARLIC CLOVES, FINELY DICED

2 BAY LEAVES

2 GREEN CAPSICUM (PEPPERS), FINELY DICED

2 TOMATOES, PEELED, SEEDED (SEE
  GLOSSARY) AND GRATED

GOOD PINCH OF SAFFRON THREADS

100 ML (3½ FL OZ) FINO SHERRY
  (SEE GLOSSARY)

300 G (10½ OZ) BOMBA RICE (SEE GLOSSARY)

12 RAW (GREEN) KING PRAWNS (SHRIMP),
  PEELED, DEVEINED AND TAILS INTACT

300 G (10½ OZ) SURF OR OTHER MEDIUM
  CLAMS (VONGOLE), PURGED

1 LEMON, CUT INTO WEDGES

FISH STOCK

1 X 1 KG (2 LB 4 OZ) WHITE-FISH HEAD,
  SUCH AS SNAPPER

1 BROWN ONION

1 WHOLE TOMATO

1 GARLIC BULB, HALVED

We wanted to offer a recipe for an everyday, simple rice dish that could be made over and over again. This has the same ingredients as one of the paellas you might find on the Costa del Sol in Andalusia, filled with mussels, prawns and calamari – tasty but developed for the tourist trade. This, however, is a more honest version. It is made in a perol pan and has a rich wet texture.

To make the fish stock, place the fish head, onion, tomato and garlic in a large stockpot with 1.5 litres (52 fl oz) of water over high heat, bring to the boil, then reduce the heat to low and simmer for 20 minutes, skimming any impurites that rise to the surface. Strain into a clean saucepan and place over low heat to keep warm. Discard the solids.

   To clean the calamari, take a hold of its tentacles and pull them out of the hood. Separate the tentacles and set aside. Gently tear off the wings and set aside. Remove the clear quill and scrape away any remaining innards. Peel the skin off. Cut the hood open along what appears to be a seam, then cut into 2 cm (⅔ inch) squares. Rinse the tentacles, wings and calamari squares and drain well.

Scrub and debeard the mussels by grasping the threads emerging from the shell and pulling back hard to the hinge. Discard the beards. Set the mussels aside.

Heat the olive oil in a 30 cm (12 inch) perol pan (see glossary) or large heavy-based saucepan over medium–high heat. Cook the calamari for 3–4 minutes each side or until golden. Season with salt while cooking. Remove from the pan and set aside.

Return the pan to medium heat. Add the onion, garlic and bay leaves and cook, stirring continuously, for 8 minutes or until the onion has browned. Add the capsicum and cook for 20 minutes or until soft. Add the tomato and saffron and cook for 15 minutes or until the tomato has cooked down and is pulpy.

Add the hot stock and sherry to the pan and bring to a simmer, then add the rice and cook, stirring, for 10 minutes.

Add the prawns and cook, without stirring, for 4 minutes. Add the clams and mussels and cook, without stirring, for 5 minutes. If after 5 minutes there are still unopened clams or mussels, prise them open with a knife, smell to check for freshness and, if there are no offensive odours, return them to the pan. Add the calamari and stir to combine everything well. Check for seasoning. Serve straight away with the lemon wedges.

WET RICE WITH LAMB RIBS & PEAS

SERVES 6

ARROZ CALDOSO CON COSTILLAS DE CORDERO

1.2 KG (2 LB 10 OZ) LAMB RIBS	2 GREEN CAPSICUM (PEPPERS), FINELY DICED
100 ML (3½ FL OZ) EXTRA VIRGIN OLIVE OIL	6 TOMATOES, PEELED, SEEDED (SEE GLOSSARY)
SEA SALT FLAKES	AND GRATED
1 BROWN ONION, FINELY DICED	300 ML (10½ FL OZ) WHITE WINE
3 GARLIC CLOVES, CHOPPED	300 G (10½ OZ) BOMBA RICE (SEE GLOSSARY)
1 TEASPOON THYME LEAVES	200 G (7 OZ) PODDED GREEN PEAS
6 BAY LEAVES	

When I was growing up, Mum kept a Spanish kitchen and a Spanish kitchen is not about extravagance. We ate lamb, but never fillet; we ate the ribs. While our Aussie neighbours were feeding ribs to their dogs, we were browning them off and using them to flavour our rice dishes for we knew that the closer to the bone the meat was, the sweeter it was. We proudly serve this dish at MoVida Aqui. Take the perol pan to the table and serve with bread and a bottle of aged Rioja.

Take a sharp knife and cut the lamb ribs between each rib to make single ribs with meat on either side of the bone. Heat 80 ml (2½ fl oz/⅓ cup) oil in a 30 cm (12 inch) perol pan (see glossary) or large heavy-based saucepan over medium–high heat and cook the ribs, in 2 batches, for 10-15 minutes or until browned all over. Season with salt while cooking. Remove from the pan and set aside.

Wipe out the pan, so that the dish does not taste too much like lamb fat, and return to medium heat. Add the remaining oil and the onion, garlic, thyme, bay leaves and season with a good pinch of salt. Cook, stirring occasionally, for 8-10 minutes or until the onion is lightly golden. Add the capsicum and cook, stirring occasionally, for 10 minutes or until softened.

Meanwhile, bring 1.5 litres (52 fl oz) of water to the boil, then reduce to a bare simmer.

Add the tomato to the onion mixture and cook for 30 minutes or until thick and pulpy. Add the wine and increase the heat to high. Allow to bubble away for a few minutes, then reduce the heat to medium–low, return the ribs to the pan and add 1 litre (35 fl oz/4 cups) of the hot water and simmer for 1 hour 10 minutes or until the ribs are tender. Add the remaining hot water, increase the heat to medium and bring to a steady simmer. Add the rice, season with salt and cook, stirring occasionally, for 15 minutes. Add the peas and cook for 4 minutes or until tender. The rice should just be a little past al dente but still firm to the bite. Serve straight away.

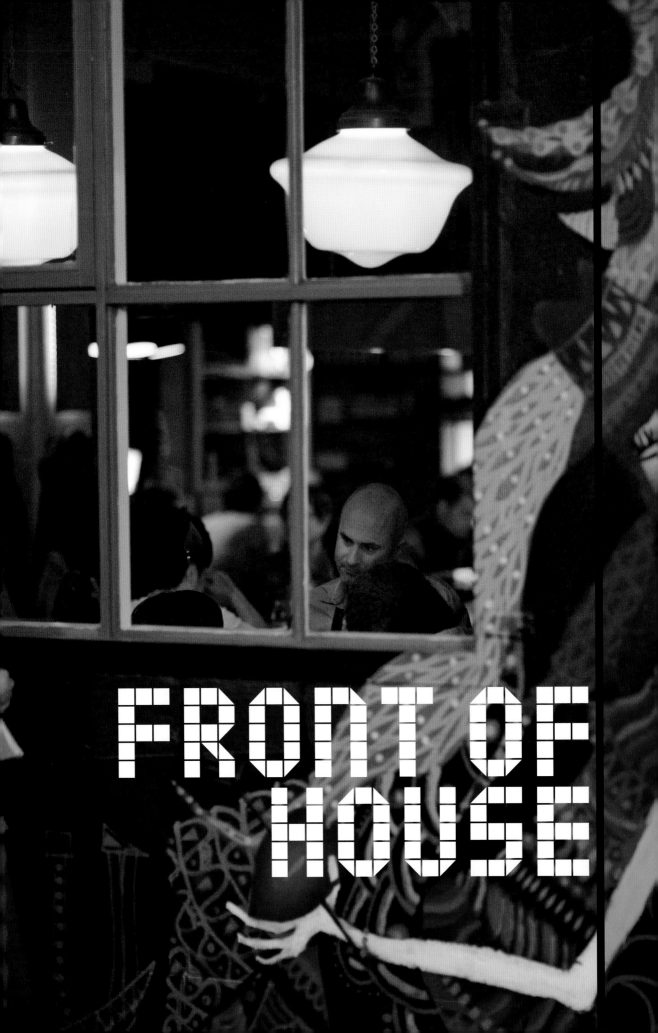

FRONT OF
HOUSE

I can wax on about the kitchen crew at MoVida Aqui. If you arrive before lunch service, you'll see them at prep chopping, cutting and boning. As the lunch rush begins, they have their heads down serving or calling orders. So as you arrive, the people you meet are not the kitchen crew but the front-of-house staff, the F.O.H. They are our public face. They combine the skills of a traffic cop, best friend, father, mother, confidant, UN mediator and stand-up comic to ensure your meal is as seamless as possible. These are our F.O.H. at MoVida.

---- ANDY MAC / My business partner and mate. He has the strongest stomach muscles — not from gym work but from belly laughs. If he finds something funny, he laughs so hard he bends in half. He also has the ability to make anyone feel welcome. I have watched him make the timid Japanese girl, guidebook in hand, peering through the door, feel like the most important person in the world within seconds. He also makes leaders of this nation and of other nations, and rock bands feel unfussed and at home.

---- DANICA / With her smooth purring voice and computer-like data system in her brain, she blends sublime professional grooming with an in-built face-recognition system that remembers who you are, what you ate and what you drank the last time you were visiting. She's old-school hospitality in a funky new form.

---- LIZ / Diamond sharp, she has worked around Australia and across the globe and has her finger on the pulse. The words 'consummate' and 'professional' were coined for her. She plays the role of matriarch, running the big F.O.H. contingent at MoVida Aqui.

---- IAIN / He's from up north of England somewhere. He looks like he should be in a comedy act — he's so bloody funny. He blends his humour with a respectfully watchful demeanour. He picks up on when your next glass of wine is needed or when your next plate should come, then they quietly arrive.

---- ALAN / Our regulars love Alan and to see him in action is a study in perception and experience. He's a 'reader'. Don't know what you want? Alan will look you up and down and pinpoint precisely what you need. If you agree, he'll have it in front of you within seconds.

---- ANDY JAC / A talent agent once came in and couldn't keep her eyes off Andy Jac. "You're so handsome," she said. "Yes that's lovely," he replied. "But let me tell you about the specials." Unaffected and dedicated to looking after his customers, Andy Jac is growing into one of Melbourne's best maîtres d'.

WET RICE WITH QUAIL & BROAD BEANS

195 G (6¾ OZ/1 CUP) DRIED WHITE LIMA
    BEANS OR GIGANTES (GIANT WHITE
    GREEK BEANS)
2 BAY LEAVES
1½ BROWN ONIONS
6 X 190 G (6¾ OZ) QUAILS
80 ML (2½ FL OZ/⅓ CUP) EXTRA VIRGIN
    OLIVE OIL
SEA SALT AND FRESHLY GROUND BLACK
    PEPPER

3 GARLIC CLOVES, FINELY DICED
1 TEASPOON THYME LEAVES
8 TOMATOES, PEELED, SEEDED
    (SEE GLOSSARY) AND GRATED
300 ML (10½ FL OZ) FINO SHERRY
    (SEE GLOSSARY)
250 G (9 OZ) BOMBA RICE (SEE GLOSSARY)
1 KG (2 LB 4 OZ) BROAD (FAVA) BEANS, PODDED
    BUT LEAVE OUTER SKINS INTACT
1 LEMON, CUT INTO WEDGES

SERVES 4–6
ARROZ CALDOSO CON CODORNIZ

Brown the skin on the quail so it caramelises and becomes a meaty little stock cube, flavouring the rice with a rich poultry hit. Make the effort to bone out the quails, so you can pick them up with your fingers and sink your teeth into them without any fuss.

You will need to begin this recipe the day before.

Place the white beans in a bowl, cover well with warm water and soak overnight. The next day, drain the beans and rinse. Place in a saucepan with the bay leaves and half an onion, cover well with water, bring to the boil, then reduce the heat to a simmer and cook for 40 minutes or until tender. Drain and discard the onion and bay leaves.

    Meanwhile, to debone the quails, working with one quail at a time, place the bird, breast-side up, on a chopping board. Slice down between the breastbone and breast meat with a sharp knife. Follow the ribcage, then along the wishbone with the blade of the knife. When you come to the wing joint, push the wing back to reveal the joint, cut the connective tissue and pop the bone out of the socket. Continue cutting down until you reach the leg joint. Carefully cut through the tendons, then pop the bone out of the socket and cut along the spine. Repeat on the other side. You should have 2 halves with leg, wing and breast, skin on. Repeat with the remaining quails. Set the quail halves aside and discard the carcasses.

    Heat 2 tablespoons of the olive oil in a 30 cm (12 inch) perol pan (see glossary) or a large heavy-based saucepan over medium–high heat. Cook the quail, skin-side down, in batches, for 3–5 minutes or until browned on one side. Season with salt and pepper, then turn over and cook the other side for 3–5 minutes or until browned. Season with salt and pepper. Remove from the pan and set aside.

    Finely dice the remaining onion. Wipe out the pan and return to medium–low heat. Add the remaining oil and cook the onion for 3 minutes. Add the garlic and thyme and cook for 10 minutes or until the onion is lightly golden. Add the tomato and cook for 12–15 minutes or until pulpy. Add the sherry, increase the heat to medium–high and bring to the boil, then return the quail to the pan, reduce the heat and simmer for 40 minutes or until the quail is just tender.

    Add 700 ml (24 fl oz) of water to the pan, increase the heat and bring to the boil, then add the rice, season with salt, reduce the heat and simmer for 10 minutes. Add the white beans and broad beans, season again with salt and simmer, stirring occasionally, for 10 minutes. The rice should have a porridge-like consistency. Check the seasoning and serve straight away with the lemon wedges.

PARTY PAELLA

SERVES 12

PAELLA DE FIESTA

1 X 1.5 KG (3 1B 5 OZ) FREE-RANGE CHICKEN

150 ML (5 FL OZ) EXTRA VIRGIN OLIVE OIL

650 G (1 LB 7 OZ) CLEANED CALAMARI, CUT
   INTO 3 CM (1¼ INCH) SQUARES

SEA SALT AND FRESHLY GROUND BLACK
   PEPPER

1 KG (2 LB 4 OZ) BROWN ONIONS, ROUGHLY
   CHOPPED (ABOUT 3 LARGE)

6 GARLIC CLOVES, FINELY CHOPPED

GOOD PINCH OF SAFFRON THREADS

6 BAY LEAVES

800 G (1 LB 12 OZ) RED CAPSICUM (PEPPERS),
   SEEDS REMOVED AND CUT INTO 1 CM
   (½ INCH) DICE

750 G (1 LB 10 OZ) GREEN CAPSICUM
   (PEPPERS), SEEDS REMOVED AND CUT INTO
   1 CM (½ INCH) DICE

8 TOMATOES, PEELED, SEEDS REMOVED
   (SEE GLOSSARY) AND GRATED

200 ML (7 FL OZ) FINO SHERRY
   (SEE GLOSSARY)

750 G (1 LB 10 OZ) BROAD (FAVA) BEANS,
   PODDED (250 G/9 OZ PODDED)

13 HANDFULS BOMBA RICE (700 G/1 LB 9 OZ)
   (SEE GLOSSARY)

3 LEMONS, CUT INTO WEDGES

The first three Christmas parties we had at MoVida involved the chefs and front-of-house cooking paella in the park on the banks of the Yarra River. We took our paella pan, our gas burner and all the ingredients we needed and set up in the afternoon sun. There were a dozen of us, all standing around the paella. We watched as the onions, then the capsicum, and then the tomatoes cooked to form the base, a jam-like mix called sofrito. Layer by layer the ingredients go in, aromatics including saffron, bay leaves and perhaps some pimentón. Then the rice, scattered across the pan like a peasant casting seed. My dad says, "One handful for the pan and then one handful for each person after that." When the rice goes in, that's the moment everyone knows dinner's not far off. There's the clatter of cutlery and crockery as everyone's hunger builds. Heat turned down and gently bubbling away, the paella looks after itself – it's never stirred. When done, it's rested before serving, covered with a clean tea (dish) towel. More wine is opened, the cloth removed and great spoonfuls of rich paella with tender chicken, pieces of calamari and dotted with beans, hit the plates along with a little of the golden socarrat or crust that forms on the base. Chef Marty who makes paella off-site for our catering gigs says: "Make sure you find level ground or the paella will not cook evenly."

To prepare the chicken, place it breast-side up on a chopping board, and slice down the breast on each side to remove the breast and wing, and thigh and leg. Remove the wings from the breasts and cut off the wings tips. Discard the carcass and wing tips (or reserve to make stock, if you wish). Cut the wings in two at the joint. Cut the breasts lengthways. Cut the smaller pieces in two and the larger in three. Trim and discard the excess skin. Remove the thighs from the legs. Remove the drumsticks from the thighs. Trim the boney end off the drumsticks and discard (or add to the carcass). Cut the drumsticks in two. Cut the thighs in three. You should have 24 pieces of chicken.

Place a 60 cm (24 inch) diameter (45 cm/17¾ inches at base) paella pan over high heat and add 100 ml (3½ fl oz) of the olive oil. Add the calamari and season with a good pinch of salt and pepper. Cook, stirring continuously, for 1½–2 minutes or until firm and caramelised. Remove from the pan, cover and set aside.

Add the chicken, season with salt and pepper and cook, stirring continuously, for 3–4 minutes or until lightly browned. Push the chicken to one side, reduce the heat to medium–low, add the remaining oil, the onion, garlic, saffron and bay leaves, season with a little salt and cook, stirring continuously, for 5 minutes or until the onion is golden. Add the capsicum and cook for 10 minutes or until soft and a jammy consistency. Mix the chicken in with the onion and capsicum.

Drain any liquid off the tomato and add to the pan. Add the sherry, increase the heat to medium–high, season with salt and pepper and cook, stirring occasionally, for 15–20 minutes, scraping the base of the pan to deglaze as the sofrito cooks. At this stage, any liquid should have reduced and the paella should look like thick, chunky jam. Add 2.6 litres (91 fl oz) of hot water from the tap, stir and continue cooking until it comes to a simmer. Return the calamari to the pan and cook for 5 minutes. Stir in the broad beans and cook for 5 minutes. Sprinkle in the rice and stir evenly through. Do not stir again. Continue cooking for 15 minutes, then remove from the heat and cover with 2 clean tea towels. Set aside for 15 minutes to steam. Divide among plates and serve with the lemon wedges.

In Spain a ración is a portion. You might order a media ración as an entrée-sized dish or a ración as a dish to share. We've taken the concept a bit further. We have developed our own internal logic that reflects our love of tapas. Generally the most exciting dishes in any restaurant will be an entrée — this is where the fun stuff happens. The main course in many establishments has become a serious affair delivering a protein and starch — thank you and good night.
---- What we've developed is a food landscape where the fun from the tapas spills over into the next course of plates. Slightly heavier with more protein, our raciones still display that love of playfulness and discovery — they just tend to be a dish that is larger, which needs to be shared. Sharing has a magic of its own. When eating a whole plate to yourself and someone asks you, "What's your dish like?" the answer is generally, "Good." But when you share a dish, you and your dining partner are experiencing exactly the same dish at the same time, so the language changes, too: "What did you think of the texture of the fish?" or "What was that spice?" You're no longer shouting across to each other from separate islands; you're on the same beach swimming in the same water.
---- A ración is a serve from a shared plate. So a '6 raciones' portion serves 6 as a main course, when accompanied by one or more other dishes. Raciones is plural of ración.

RACIONES
SHARE PLATES

SLOW-COOKED EGG WITH BROAD BEANS, JAMÓN IBÉRICO & TRUFFLE

4 RACIONES

HUEVO CON IBÉRICO, HABAS Y TRUFA

4 EGGS	FINE SEA SALT
50 G (1¾ OZ) JAMÓN IBÉRICO FAT, FINELY DICED	EXTRA VIRGIN OLIVE OIL, FOR DRIZZLING
1.5 KG (3 LB 5 OZ) BROAD (FAVA) BEANS, PODDED BUT LEAVE THE OUTER SKINS INTACT (SEE NOTE)	8 THIN SLICES JAMÓN IBÉRICO, FOR SERVING
	8 G (¼ OZ) FRESH BLACK TRUFFLE
2 THICK SLICES JAMÓN IBÉRICO (SEE GLOSSARY), FINELY DICED	

The flavours of truffles and broad beans work so well together. One is the food of the rich, the other a staple of the poor; together they have the ability to completely fill your sense of flavour without treading on each other's toes.

Fill a saucepan with water and place on a heat diffuser over low heat. Heat to 65°C (149°F). Check the temperature with a digital thermometer. If the temperature rises above 65°C move the pan off the heat a little until it stabilises at 65°C. Cook the eggs in the water bath for 75 minutes. Remove from the pan. Remove the top quarter of each eggshell with an egg clacker (see page 110) and discard. If you don't have an egg clacker, use a serrated knife to slowly cut through the shell. Place the eggs in an egg carton until ready to serve.

Meanwhile, place the jamón fat in a small saucepan over very low heat and allow the fat to render for 20 minutes but do not allow to brown.

Meanwhile, bring a small saucepan of salted water to the boil over high heat. Blanch the broad beans for 20 seconds or until just tender. Drain and refresh in iced water. Drain again. Peel off the outer skins and set aside.

Strain the rendered fat into a small clean saucepan and discard the solids. Place the pan over low heat. Add the diced jamón and broad beans, cover and cook for 1 minute or until warmed through.

To serve, spoon the broad bean mixture and pan juices onto warmed serving plates. Delicately slide each cooked egg out of its shell and over the broad bean mixture. Season the egg with salt and drizzle over the olive oil. Arrange 2 slices of jamón over each egg and, using a Microplane grater, finely grate over some truffle. Serve straight away.

NOTE: You will need about 500 g (1 lb 2 oz) podded broad beans.

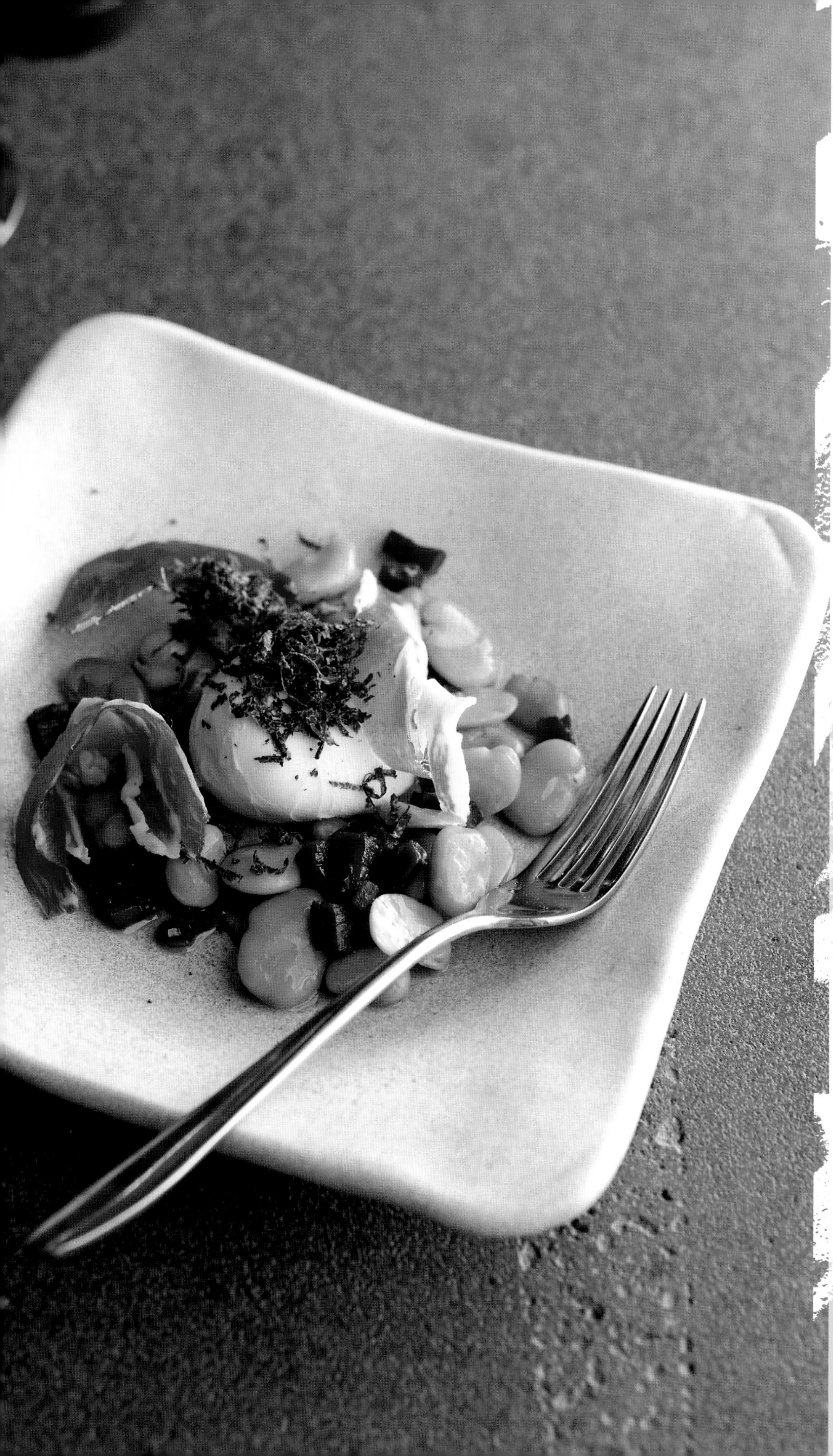

OCTOPUS

PULPO

3 RED CAPSICUM (PEPPERS)	1 KG (2 LB 4 OZ) KIPFLER POTATOES, UNPEELED
1 BULB GARLIC	SMOKED SWEET PAPRIKA (PIMENTÓN),
2 TABLESPOONS EXTRA VIRGIN OLIVE OIL, PLUS	TO TASTE
EXTRA FOR DRIZZLING	FINELY CHOPPED PARSLEY, FOR GARNISHING
COOKING SALT	SEA SALT FLAKES
1 KG (2 LB 4 OZ/ABOUT 3) OCTOPUS TENTACLES	

This recipe is as close to the traditional Galician home method of cooking octopus that is possible in a restaurant. In Spanish bars and restaurants, typically, the prepared octopus and potato sits in the fridge and is warmed before serving. This makes it a great dish to cook if entertaining.

You will need to begin this recipe the day before.

Preheat the oven to 180°C (350°F/Gas 4). Place the capsicum and garlic in a small roasting tray, drizzle with the olive oil and season with a pinch of cooking salt. Roast for 20 minutes, then remove the garlic and set aside. Continue roasting the capsicum for another 15 minutes or until the skin is charred. Remove the capsicum, place in a bowl and cover with plastic wrap to lightly steam; this will make them easier to peel. Reserve any cooking juices in the tray. When cool enough to handle, peel away the skin from the capsicum and discard along with the stalks and seeds. Place the capsicum flesh in a blender. Squeeze the garlic cloves into the blender, add the reserved cooking juices, season with paprika and blend for 1 minute or until smooth. Transfer to a bowl, season with 1 teaspoon of salt, cover and set aside.

Meanwhile, bring a large saucepan of fresh water to a rapid boil. Rinse the octopus under cold running water. Using a pair of tongs, plunge the octopus into the boiling water for 15 seconds, then remove. Allow the water to return to the boil, then repeat plunging 3 more times, ensuring the water returns to the boil between each immersion. Return all the octopus to the boiling water and leave in the pan. Reduce the heat to a bare simmer and cook the octopus for 30–40 minutes or until tender. To test if it's ready, insert a small knife into a tentacle; it shouldn't meet much resistance and the outside layer should be pink and intact. Remove the octopus from the pan and set aside to cool.

Increase the heat to high and bring the water back to the boil. Add the potatoes, reduce the heat to a simmer and cook for 30 minutes or until tender. Drain and, when cool enough to handle, peel.

Cut the tentacles into 13 cm (5 inch) lengths. Place an octopus length and 2 potatoes in a high-density plastic bag with 1 tablespoon of the capsicum paste and season with cooking salt, so you will have 6 bags in total. Follow our steps on sous-vide cooking (see page 123). Vacuum seal the bags, then refrigerate for 24 hours.

The next day, cook the octopus in a water bath at 80°C (176°F) for 10–15 minutes or until heated through. Remove the bags from the water. Slice the octopus crossways into 2 cm (¾ inch) thick rounds. Slice the potatoes crossways into 1.5 cm (⅝ inch) thick rounds, too.

To serve, arrange the potato on warmed serving plates. Place the rounds of octopus on top in a random fashion. Sprinkle with a little paprika, garnish with some parsley, drizzle with a little olive oil and serve straight away.

PULPO
THE OCTOPUS

We love pulpo. He has become one of our icons at MoVida Aqui. There's a brand of canned octopus in Spain that has the best design. It looks more like a toy or a fun range of chocolates. When we were thinking about how Aqui should look, we came up with the idea of decorating the interior of the building with fun designs of some of the typical animals we planned to serve. One of our kitchen hands, Tim, is a graphic designer. He took the design from said brand of canned octopus and turned it into a cartoon character. He and his team also developed Gamba the Prawn, Cabra the Goat, Ostra the Oyster and Cochinillo the Piglet. I love them all, but between you and me, Pulpo is my favourite.

BRAISED PORK NECK WITH OLOROSO SHERRY & PRUNES

6-8 RACIONES

ESTOFADO DE CERDO

1 KG (2 LB 4 OZ) PORK NECK	1 BAY LEAF
90 ML (3 FL OZ) EXTRA VIRGIN OLIVE OIL	500 G (1 LB 2 OZ) PITTED PRUNES
SEA SALT AND FRESHLY GROUND BLACK PEPPER	1.1 LITRE (38½ FL OZ) OLOROSO SHERRY (SEE GLOSSARY)
1 BROWN ONION, DICED	300 ML (10½ FL OZ) CHICKEN STOCK
1 GARLIC CLOVE, CHOPPED	110 G (3¾ OZ/½ CUP) CASTER (SUPERFINE) SUGAR
1 TEASPOON THYME LEAVES, FINELY CHOPPED	

This slow-cooked pork, sticky and sweet, falls apart under your fork. Chef Robbo shows his understanding of Spanish food here. Take a lesser-loved cut, cook it in the proper manner with the food around you and the result is a truly delicious dish that has completely transcended the ingredients.

Cut the pork into 4 cm x 4 cm (1½ inch x 1½ inch) chunks. Heat 60 ml (2 fl oz/¼ cup) of the olive oil in a large heavy-based saucepan over medium–high heat. Season the pork with salt and pepper and cook, in 2–3 batches, for about 5 minutes or until browned all over. Remove the pork from the pan and set aside.

Wipe out the pan and return to medium–low heat. Add the remaining oil. Add the onion, garlic, thyme and bay leaf and cook, stirring occasionally, for 15 minutes or until the onion is soft and translucent.

Finely chop 300 g (10½ oz) of the prunes until they resemble a smooth paste. Add to the onion mixture and cook for 5 minutes, stirring occasionally so the prunes don't stick to the base of the pan and burn.

Return the pork and any juices to the pan along with 600 ml (21 fl oz) of the sherry and the stock and stir to combine. Increase the heat to high and bring to the boil. Skim off any impurities, reduce the heat to low and simmer, covered, stirring occasionally, for 1–1½ hours or until the pork is tender. Check the seasoning.

When the pork is nearly ready, place the sugar and remaining sherry in a deep-sided saucepan over high heat, stir to dissolve the sugar and bring to the boil, then reduce the heat to low, add the remaining prunes and cook for 8 minutes or until the prunes are plump and have absorbed most of the liquid. Do not overcook the prunes as they will start to break up and become mushy. Add to the pork mixture, stir gently to combine and serve straight away.

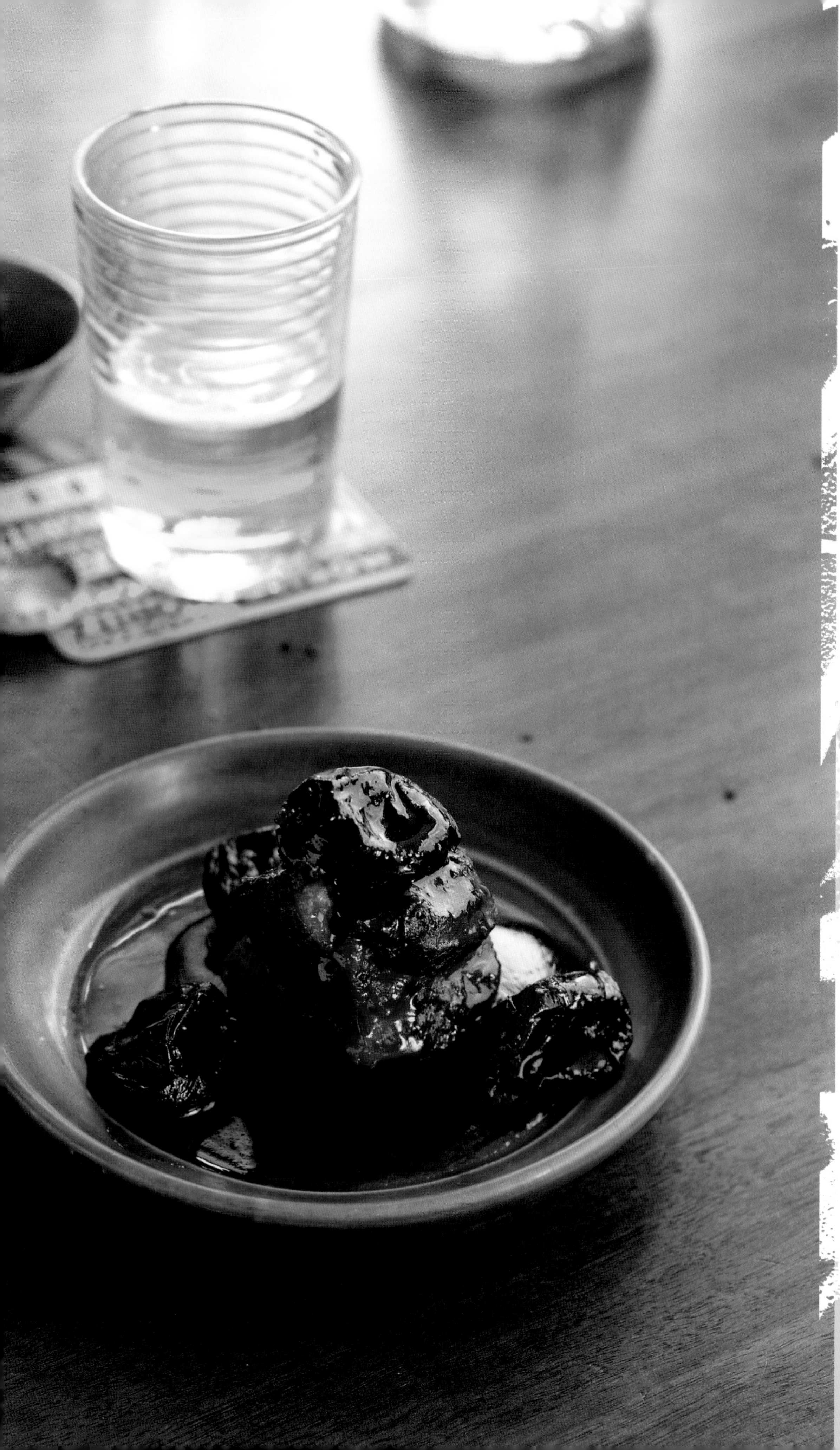

SPICY SEVILLE PORK CRACKLING

800 G (1 LB 12 OZ) PORK BELLY, SKIN ON	2 TABLESPOONS SEA SALT FLAKES	
315 G (11 OZ/1 CUP) ROCK SALT	SUNFLOWER OR VEGETABLE OIL,	
1 TABLESPOON CUMIN SEEDS	FOR DEEP-FRYING	
1 TABLESPOON FENNEL SEEDS	10 GARLIC CLOVES, UNPEELED	
1 TEASPOON SMOKED HOT PAPRIKA (PIMENTÓN)	12 SPRIGS ROSEMARY	
1 TEASPOON FRESHLY GROUND BLACK PEPPER		

12 RACIONES
CHICHARRONES DE SEVILLA

This classic bar snack from Seville is extremely addictive. Small slices of pork belly are salted, then deep-fried. This version comes from a butcher at the Mercado de La Encarnación in Seville. He serves them in a paper cone with pieces of fried garlic and rosemary. Our elaboration is a blend of Andalusian spices sprinkled over the hot chicharrones. Serve with a cold beer and enjoy with your cardiologist.

Cut the pork into 5 cm x 2 cm (2 inch x ¾ inch) lardons and place in a bowl with the rock salt. Mix well and allow to sit at room temperature for 3 hours. This will draw out any excess moisture.

Wash the pork in cold running water to remove the salt. Place the pork in a large saucepan, cover with water and bring to the boil over high heat, then reduce the heat to a simmer and cook for 2½ hours or until tender. Drain well and pat very dry with paper towel.

Meanwhile, preheat the oven to 180°C (350°F/Gas 4). Place the cumin and fennel seeds on a baking tray lined with baking paper and roast for 5 minutes or until aromatic. Allow to cool, then grind in a spice grinder or pound in a mortar and pestle. Add the paprika, pepper, sea salt and combine. Set aside.

Fill a large heavy-based saucepan or deep-fryer one-third full with oil and heat to 160°C (315°F) or until a cube of bread dropped into the oil takes 30–35 seconds to turn golden. Lightly crush the garlic cloves so they don't explode when cooked. Deep-fry the garlic for 7 minutes or until deep golden, then add the rosemary and continue frying for another minute. Remove and drain on paper towel. Increase the oil temperature to 165°C (329°F) and deep-fry the pork, in batches, for 15 minutes or until crisp and golden. Please note that on the odd occasion, if not dry enough, a pork piece may explode, so take extra care. We think it is worth the risk! Skim off any floating debris between each batch. Drain on paper towel. Season while hot with the spice mix and toss with the garlic and rosemary. Serve straight away.

AIR-DRIED WAGYU WITH TRUFFLED POTATO FOAM & EGG

6–8 RACIONES

CECINA

TRUFFLED POTATO FOAM

- 2 LARGE (ABOUT 250 G/9 OZ EACH) WHITE-SKINNED POTATOES, WASHED
- 2 TEASPOONS SEA SALT FLAKES
- 175 ML (6 FL OZ) MILK
- 175 ML (6 FL OZ) POURING (SINGLE) CREAM
- 50 G (1¾ OZ) UNSALTED BUTTER
- 2½ TABLESPOONS BLACK TRUFFLE PASTE (SEE NOTES)
- 1 TEASPOON AGAR AGAR POWDER

POACHED EGGS

- 6–8 EGGS, AT FRIDGE TEMPERATURE
- 75 ML (2⅗ FL OZ) WHITE WINE VINEGAR

TO SERVE

- 250 G (9 OZ) AIR-DRIED WAGYU, CUT INTO 1 MM (1/32 INCH) THICK SLICES
- BLACK SEA SALT FLAKES, FOR GARNISHING
- EXTRA VIRGIN OLIVE OIL, FOR DRIZZLING

This dish won Dish of The Year from *The Age Good Food Guide* when we first put it on the menu in 2007 and we have never been able to take it off since without suffering cries of protestation from customers, especially those from overseas who have read about it and made it part of their Melbourne food odyssey itinerary. You'll need a cream canister to make the foam but apart from that it is deceptively easy.

To make the truffled potato foam, peel and cut the potatoes into 5 cm (2 inch) cubes. Place in a saucepan, cover with water and add 1 teaspoon of the salt. Bring to a boil over high heat, then reduce the heat to medium and cook for 15 minutes or until tender. Drain well and, while still warm, pass through a potato ricer or food mill into a bowl.

Heat the milk, cream and butter in a small saucepan over medium heat until the butter has melted. Reduce the heat to low, add the potato, truffle paste, agar agar and remaining salt and mix well. Heat to 60°C (140°F), then, working as quickly as possible, using a broad-spouted funnel, pour the mixture into a cream canister and charge with 2 soda bulbs (see glossary). Keep heated by placing in a warm water bath at 55°C–60°C (131°F–140°F) and allow to stand for 1 hour.

Meanwhile, make the poached eggs. Bring 2 litres (70 fl oz) of water and the vinegar to the boil. Swirl a spoon in the pan to create a whirlpool, then break an egg into a cup and slide it into the centre of the whirlpool. Reduce the heat to a simmer and poach for 3 minutes. Remove with a slotted spoon, drain on a tea (dish) towel and keep warm. Repeat with the remaining eggs. To speed up the process, you can bring another pan of water and vinegar to the boil and poach another egg at the same time or, if you are confident, you can poach 2 eggs together in the same pan.

To serve, neatly arrange the slices of wagyu over warmed individual serving plates. Spray a golf-ball-sized amount of foam over the wagyu and place an egg on top. Finish with a sprinkle of black sea salt and a drizzle of olive oil.

NOTES: Black truffle paste is available from gourmet food stores. You can substitute truffle oil to taste — about 2 teaspoons will be sufficient.

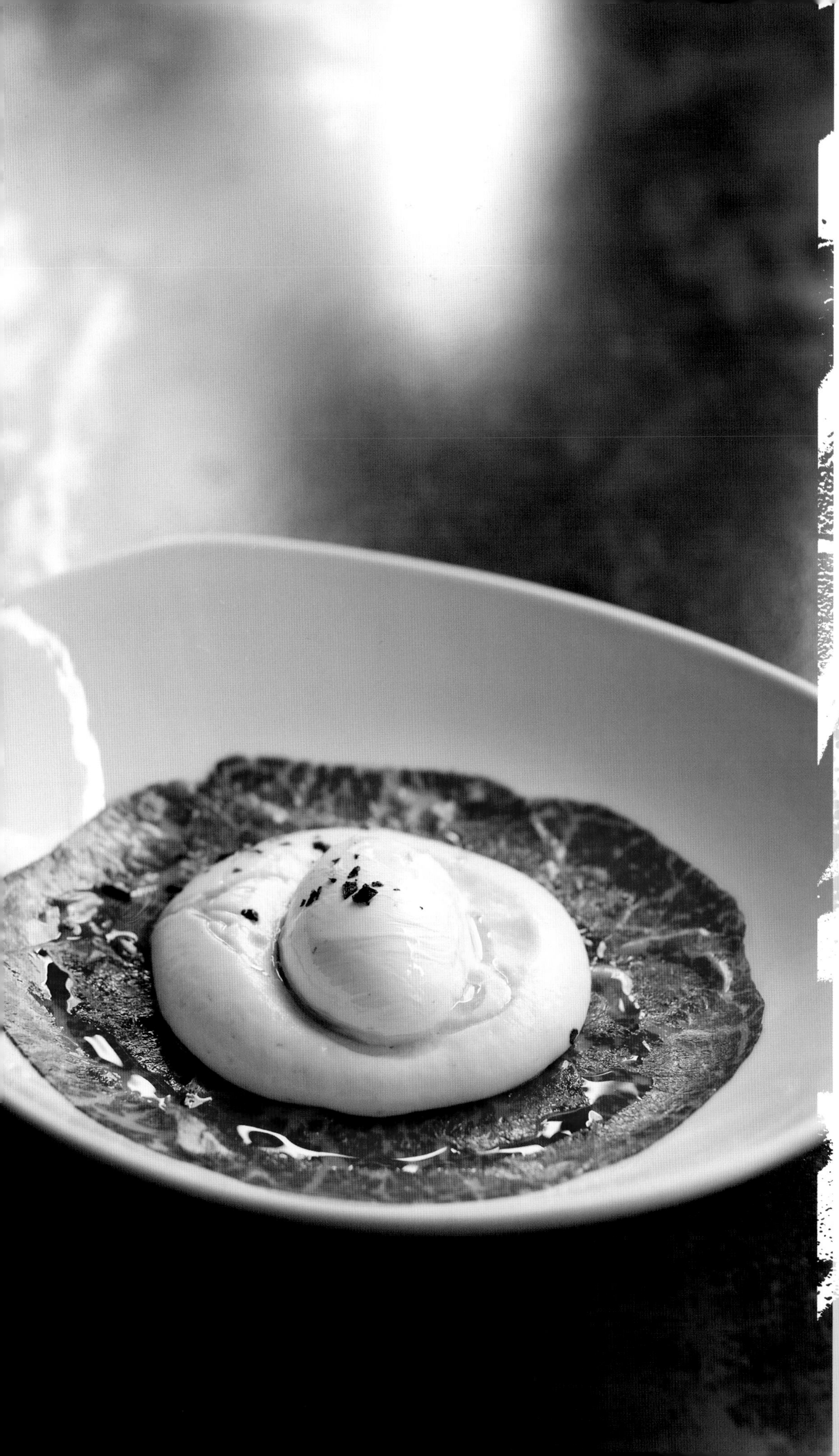

PORK & PEPPER CATALAN SAUSAGE WITH BLACK BEANS & PIQUILLO PEPPERS

SERVES 6

BUTIFARRA

BUTIFARRA

8 GARLIC CLOVES

80 ML (2½ FL OZ/⅓ CUP) FINO SHERRY
  (SEE GLOSSARY)

1.5 KG (3 LB 5 OZ) PORK SHOULDER

500 G (1 LB 2 OZ) TOCINO (SEE GLOSSARY)

38 G (1¼ OZ) FINE SEA SALT

30 G (1 OZ) FRESHLY GROUND BLACK PEPPER

16 G (⅝ OZ) DRIED OREGANO

3 METRE-LONG X 38 MM WIDE
  (9 FEET 10½ INCHES X 1½ INCH) SAUSAGE
  CASINGS (SEE NOTES)

BUTTER, FOR COOKING

BLACK BEANS

200 G (7 OZ) PIECE OF TOCINO, SPECK OR
  SMOKY BACON

400 G (14 OZ) DRIED BLACK (TURTLE) BEANS,
  SOAKED OVERNIGHT IN WATER

1 BROWN ONION, HALVED

1 RIPE WHOLE TOMATO

1 CARROT, CUT INTO 4 PIECES

4 BAY LEAVES

1 RED CAPSICUM (PEPPER), HALVED, STALK
  AND SEEDS REMOVED

SEA SALT FLAKES

12 PIMIENTOS DE PIQUILLO (SEE GLOSSARY),
  DRAINED

MOJO

1 TEASPOON FENNEL SEEDS

1 TEASPOON CUMIN SEEDS

1 CUP CORIANDER (CILANTRO) LEAVES

1 CUP CURLY PARSLEY LEAVES

2 GARLIC CLOVES

2½ TABLESPOONS CHARDONNAY VINEGAR

100 ML (3½ FL OZ) EXTRA VIRGIN OLIVE OIL,
  PLUS EXTRA FOR SERVING

SEA SALT AND FRESHLY GROUND BLACK PEPPER

I originally wanted to call my first restaurant Butifarra. Thankfully friends talked me out of it. Butifarra is the quintessential Catalan sausage. It's big, porky, full of pepper and delicious. Chef James makes ours twice weekly and serves them with beans. It's a good idea to have a mincer and sausage-making machine on hand (although we have supplied alternative methods).

You will need to begin this recipe 3 days ahead.

To make the butifarra, you should keep in mind the 3 rules of sausage making: cool, clean and quick. Work with cold meat, make sure your hands and surfaces are clean and don't leave the meat around to warm up. Purée the garlic and sherry in a small blender or pound in a mortar and pestle, then transfer to a large stainless steel bowl.

Trim the pork of any bits of gristle or bone and discard but do not trim off the fat. Cut the pork into 5 cm x 3 cm (2 inch x 1¼ inch) chunks to facilitate the mincing. Mince two-thirds of the pork using the coarse plate, then mince the remaining pork using the medium plate. Add both minces to the bowl. (If you don't have a mincer, ask your butcher to do this for you.)

210

Using a sharp knife, dice the pork fat into 3 mm (⅛ inch) cubes and add to the bowl with the salt, pepper and oregano. Using your hands, mix well for 5–10 minutes or until the fat starts clinging to your hands. Cover and refrigerate overnight.

The next day, wash the sausage casings of excess salt and soak in water for 1 hour before using. Place the pork mixture in a sausage-making machine or sausage pump and slide the entire length of casing onto the nozzle of the sausage attachment. (If you don't have this equipment, fill a large piping bag fitted with a nozzle with the pork mixture.) Allow a little pork mixture to enter the casing to force out the air that would otherwise fill the casing. Stop. Tie off the end as one would a child's balloon. Continue stuffing the mixture into the casings. Make sure the stuffed casing is neither too flaccid nor too tight or the sausage may burst. When you have filled the casing, tie off the end. Twist the length of sausage into 15 cm (6 inch) long links, twisting each new link in the opposite direction. You should end up with 15 sausages but you will only need 6 for this recipe (see notes). Using a small S-hook, hang the sausages, uncovered, from the top shelf of the fridge over a bowl for 48 hours to allow the flavours to meld. You may need to clear a space in your fridge to ensure there is no cross-contamination.

On the day of serving, make the black beans. Dice the tocino into 3 mm (⅛ inch) cubes and place in a large, heavy-based saucepan over medium–high heat with the black beans, onion, tomato, carrot, bay leaves, capsicum and 1.5 litres (52 fl oz) of water. Cover with a cartouche (see notes) and cook for 1 hour 10 minutes or until the beans are tender. Drain, then remove the onion, tomato, carrot, bay leaf and capsicum and discard. Season with salt.

Meanwhile, heat a barbecue char-grill plate or char-grill pan to high. Char-grill the peppers for 1–2 minutes each side or until nice grill marks form and there is a charry aroma. Cut into 2.5 cm (1 inch) thick slices. Add to the bean mixture and gently mix. Set aside and keep warm.

Meanwhile, make the mojo. Preheat the oven to 180°C (350°F/Gas 4). Spread the fennel and cumin seeds evenly over a baking tray and roast for 5 minutes or until aromatic. Cool slightly, then tip into a blender. Add the coriander, parsley, garlic, vinegar and olive oil, season with a pinch of salt and pepper and blend for 1 minute or until smooth. Set aside.

To serve, increase the oven temperature to 200°C (400°F/Gas 6). Place 6 sausages on a tray, dot with a little butter and bake, turning occasionally, for 8–10 minutes or until golden and cooked through. Reheat the beans and spoon onto warmed individual serving plates. Slice each sausage on the diagonal into 3 even-sized portions. Arrange the sausages on the beans and spoon over dollops of the mojo sauce. Drizzle with a little oil and sprinkle with salt.

NOTES: To make a cartouche, cut a circle of baking paper just slightly larger than the diameter of the saucepan and place directly on the surface of the ingredients.

Extra sausages can be frozen, raw, for up to 2 months.

TERRINA $19.5
RABBIT TERRINE W
BEETROOT PUREE

TORTILLA
spanner crab, leek $25
Majorero cheese, fresh truffle (

BEEF CHEEK & PIQUILLO PEPPER PIE

EMPANADA DE BUEY Y PIQUILLOS

BEEF FILLING

- 3 X 300 G (10½ OZ) BEEF CHEEKS
- SEA SALT AND FRESHLY GROUND BLACK PEPPER
- 60 ML (2 FL OZ/¼ CUP) OLIVE OIL
- 2 CARROTS, ROUGHLY CHOPPED
- ½ BROWN ONION, SLICED
- ½ GARLIC BULB, HALVED
- 250 ML (9 FL OZ/1 CUP) PEDRO XIMÉNEZ SHERRY (SEE GLOSSARY)
- 250 ML (9 FL OZ/1 CUP) FULL-BODIED RED WINE
- 2 BAY LEAVES
- 1½ TABLESPOONS THYME LEAVES
- ½ TEASPOON FINE SEA SALT

DOUGH

- 375 G (13 OZ/2½ CUPS) PLAIN (ALL-PURPOSE) FLOUR, PLUS EXTRA FOR DUSTING
- 375 G (13 OZ/2½ CUPS) SELF-RAISING (SELF-RISING) FLOUR
- SEA SALT FLAKES
- 375 ML (13 FL OZ/1½ CUPS) EXTRA VIRGIN OLIVE OIL
- 375 ML (13 FL OZ/1½ CUPS) FINO SHERRY (SEE GLOSSARY), PLUS AN EXTRA SPLASH

TO ASSEMBLE

- 1 X 265 G (9½ OZ) JAR PIMIENTOS DE PIQUILLO (SEE GLOSSARY), DRAINED
- 1 EGG, LIGHTLY BEATEN

Chef Marty (see page 30) puts on this rustic dish at La Terraza or serves it up when he's catering off-site. It's good-quality fast food, classically Spanish and transports well. It works well in a picnic hamper and can be cut into smaller portions, making it the perfect finger food.

To make the beef filling, trim the cheeks of sinew and silver skin. Season well with salt and pepper. Heat half of the olive oil in a large heavy-based saucepan over high heat. Cook the cheeks for 2 minutes each side or until browned. Remove from the pan and set aside.

Wipe out the pan and return to medium–high heat. Add the remaining oil and when very hot, add the carrot, onion and garlic and cook for 10–12 minutes or until well browned. Stir in the sherry, wine, bay leaves, thyme, fine sea salt and 250 ml (9 fl oz/1 cup) of water. Reduce the heat to as low as possible, add the cheeks, cover and cook for 3–4 hours or until the cheeks are beginning to fall apart. Remove the cheeks and set aside to cool.

Strain the cooking liquid, reserve the beef, discard the remaining solids, then return the strained liquid to the pan and cook over medium–low heat for 8 minutes or until reduced to a glaze-like consistency.

Shred the cheeks into a bowl and mix in 100 ml (3½ fl oz) of the reduced glaze, or as much as needed to just lightly coat the meat, but take care as too much sauce will make the pastry soft. Cover and set aside.

Meanwhile, make the dough. Sift the flours together with a pinch of salt into a large bowl and make a well in the centre. Pour the olive oil and sherry into the well and mix together until a soft dough forms. Briefly knead for a minutes or so until the dough comes together and is elastic. You'll know it's ready when it feels heavier and wetter than a normal dough. If it seems a little dry, add another splash of sherry. Form into a ball, cover with plastic wrap and leave at room temperature for 30 minutes.

Preheat the oven to 180°C (350°F/Gas 4). Line a 34 cm x 26 cm x 3 cm (13½ inch x 10½ inch x 1¼ inch) baking tray with baking paper.

Divide the dough into 2 pieces. On a lightly floured surface, roll out one piece to about 3 mm (⅛ inch) thick to fit the tray. Line the tray with the pastry. Allow to rest for 10 minutes.

Bake the base for 8 minutes or until crisp. Allow to cool on the tray.

Roll out the remaining pastry to about 3 mm (⅛ inch) thick to form a lid for the base. Allow to rest for 10 minutes.

To assemble, cut the pimientos at the seams and open out to form flat triangular pieces. Arrange them, edge to edge, in a single layer over the pastry base. Spoon the beef cheek mixture over the top and use the back of a spoon to smooth into an even layer. Cover with the pastry lid and neatly trim the edges, allowing a little excess for shrinkage. Press along the edges to seal. Bake for 10 minutes, then brush with a little of the beaten egg. Continue baking for another 25 minutes or until golden and cooked through. Cool in the tray slightly to just warm, then cut into pieces and serve straight away.

POACHED WAGYU FILLET WITH BLACK & WHITE GARLIC & 'FAT FROM HEAVEN'

6 RACIONES

BUEY CON TOCINO DE CIELO

POACHED WAGYU

- 1 X 600 G (1 LB 5 OZ) PIECE OF WAGYU ROST
  BIFF, MARBLE SCORE 6-PLUS (SEE NOTES)
- 1 TEASPOON THYME LEAVES
- 2 BAY LEAVES
- 2 TABLESPOONS EXTRA VIRGIN OLIVE OIL,
  PLUS EXTRA FOR DRIZZLING

TOCINO DE CIELO

- 200 G (7 OZ) CASTER (SUPERFINE) SUGAR
- 85 G (3 OZ) MALTOSE (SEE NOTES)
- 1 EGG
- 8 EGG YOLKS
- 3 TABLESPOONS STORE-BOUGHT
  HORSERADISH CREAM
- FINE SEA SALT AND FRESHLY GROUND
  WHITE PEPPER

POTATO CRISPS

- 2 SEBAGO POTATOES
- 2 TEASPOONS CORNFLOUR (CORNSTARCH)
- 2½ X 2 G (⅟₁₆ OZ) GELATINE SHEETS
  (GOLD STRENGTH)
- 60 G (2¼ OZ) UNSALTED BUTTER, MELTED
- SEA SALT FLAKES

TO SERVE

- 12 BLACK GARLIC CLOVES (SEE NOTES)
- 12 PICKLED GARLIC CLOVES (SEE GLOSSARY)
- BLACK SEA SALT, FOR GARNISHING
- ⅔ CUP FINELY CHOPPED CHIVES

When you're in a group working on new recipes you have to keep an open mind and trust other chefs' inspiration. It's a time when you're free to take risks and try new combinations. Who would ever have thought that tocino de cielo ('fat from heaven'), a classic Spanish sweet custard, would marry with rare beef and pickled and fermented garlic? It works brilliantly.

To make the poached wagyu, place the beef, herbs and olive oil in a high-density plastic bag. Follow our steps on sous-vide cooking (see page 123). Vacuum seal the bags and cook in a water bath at 60°C (140°F) for 1 hour 10 minutes. Remove the bag from the water bath and place in iced water to cool down as quickly as possible. Remove from the water and refrigerate until ready to use. You can refrigerate for up to 3 days.

To make the tocino de cielo, preheat the oven to 170°C (325°F/Gas 3). Place 110 g (3¾ oz/½ cup) of the sugar in a small saucepan over medium heat and cook, without stirring, for 12 minutes, then as the sugar starts to change colour, stir with a metal spoon and continue cooking for 10 minutes or until deep golden and smells like toffee, but be careful not to burn it or you will have to start again. Pour into a 15 cm x 12 cm x 4 cm (6 inch x 4½ inch x 1½ inch) heatproof tray and swirl to coat the base. Allow the caramel to cool, then set aside.

Meanwhile, place the remaining sugar, maltose and 180 ml (6 fl oz) of water in a small saucepan over medium heat. Stir until the sugar dissolves, then bring to a simmer and cook for 15 minutes or until reduced and thickened slightly. Allow to cool down until lukewarm. Lightly whisk the egg and egg yolks in a bowl, working very gently trying not to incorporate air into the mixture.

While whisking gently, slowly pour the lukewarm sugar syrup into the egg mixture. Add the horseradish cream, season with a good pinch of salt and a small pinch of pepper and mix in. Pour this custard mixture over the caramel and place the tray in a roasting tray. Place in the oven and pour in enough hot water to fill the roasting tray until it is at the same level as the top of the custard. Bake for 40 minutes or until firm. Remove from the water bath and allow to cool, then cover with plastic wrap and refrigerate for 3 hours. This will make more than you will need but it allows for breakages when cutting and plating this delicate mixture.

To make the potato crisps, peel the potato and grate into a bowl. Sprinkle over the cornflour and mix well to coat. Spread in an even layer in the top of a double boiler or steamer basket lined with baking paper. Cover and cook over a saucepan of simmering water for 2–3 minutes or until just softened; the potato should be al dente.

Meanwhile, soften the gelatine sheets in a large bowl of water for 2 minutes. Squeeze out the excess water. Place the gelatine in a bowl, add the warm melted butter and a good pinch of salt and stir until the gelatine has dissolved. Add the warm grated potato and mix well to form a sticky dough.

Place a double-layered square of plastic wrap on a bench. Take the dough and, starting 2 cm (¾ inch) in, place it along the edge closest to you, patting it out to make a rough 3 cm (1¼ inch) diameter sausage shape, making sure there is a good 3 cm (1¼ inches) clear at either end. Pinch either end of the plastic wrap and roll up the dough tightly. Secure the ends and roll in a few more layers of plastic wrap to make it watertight. Place in iced water for 10 minutes or until the gelatine sets, then freeze for 2–3 hours or until frozen hard.

Preheat the oven to 180°C (350°F/Gas 4). Remove the plastic wrap from the log and, using a very sharp knife, slice it into 3 mm (⅛ inch) thick rounds. Place the slices in a single layer on a baking tray lined with baking paper and bake for 40 minutes or until crisp and golden.

To serve, remove the wagyu from the bag and place on a chopping board. Thinly slice the beef and arrange on individual serving plates. Dip the base of the tocino de cielo mould briefly in warm water, then invert onto a lipped tray to catch any runny caramel. Dice the tocino into 5 mm (¼ inch) cubes and gently scatter 8–10 cubes over the wagyu. Cut each black and pickled garlic cloves crossways into 3 pieces and scatter over the wagyu. Drizzle 1 tablespoon of the caramel from the tocino de cielo over the wagyu, then drizzle with a little oil. Place 10 potato crisps upright on each plate. Sprinkle with the black salt and chives and serve straight away.

NOTES: Wagyu rost biff is the elongated part of the rump. You will need a piece that is about 8 cm (3¼ inches) in diameter for the entire length. Order it in advance from your butcher and ask them to cut it for you.

Maltose is a type of sugar derived from barley. It is used extensively in the food industry and is available online.

Black garlic is garlic that has undergone a fermentation process that transforms it from pungent and bitey to rich and mellow. It's available from gourmet food stores, select greengrocers and farmers' markets.

DUCK LIVERS WITH CHANTERELLES & MAJORCAN PASTRIES

700 G (1 LB 9 OZ) DUCK LIVERS	80 ML (2½ FL OZ/⅓ CUP) MILD HONEY
100 ML (3½ FL OZ) PEDRO XIMÉNEZ SHERRY	6 ENSAIMADAS (SEE PAGE 24)
(SEE GLOSSARY)	1½ TABLESPOONS CASTER (SUPERFINE) SUGAR
125 ML (4 FL OZ/½ CUP) EXTRA VIRGIN OLIVE OIL	200 G (7 OZ) CHANTERELLE, OYSTER
2 BROWN ONIONS, THINLY SLICED	OR KING BROWN MUSHROOMS
PINK SEA SALT (SEE GLOSSARY)	1 TEASPOON THYME LEAVES
500 ML (17 FL OZ/2 CUPS) OLOROSO SHERRY	1 TABLESPOON FINELY CHOPPED PARSLEY
(SEE GLOSSARY)	

6 RACIONES

ENSAIMADAS CON HÍGADO DE PATO

Shared plates means that people can try a dish without investing their whole main course in it. Take these sweet livers with mushrooms, a dish inspired by Paco Guzmán at his restaurant in Barcelona. We take an ensaimada, sprinkle sugar on it and blowtorch it till bittersweet and fill it with livers soaked in sherry. Everyone who tries it loves it, even if they're not sure at first.

You will need to begin this recipe the day before.

Trim any sinew from the livers. Cut each into 3 equal pieces. Place in a non-reactive dish, pour over the Pedro Ximénez sherry, cover and refrigerate overnight.

The next day, heat 60 ml (2 fl oz/¼ cup) of the oil in a heavy-based saucepan over a medium–high heat, add the onion, season with salt, reduce the heat to low and cook, stirring occasionally, for 20 minutes or until the onion has softened.

Place the oloroso sherry and honey in a heavy-based saucepan and bring to a simmer over medium heat. Cook for 10–15 minutes or until reduced by half. Set aside.

Cut the ensaimadas in half and sprinkle the tops and bottoms with the sugar. Caramelise with a kitchen blowtorch or under a hot grill (broiler) for 30 seconds or until the sugar has melted and slightly burned. Set aside.

Heat 2 teaspoons of the oil in a large non-stick frying pan over high heat and cook the livers, in 3 separate batches, for 45 seconds each side or until sealed, seasoning with salt while cooking. Remove from the pan and place in a bowl. Drizzle with 2 tablespoons of the oloroso glaze and cover with aluminium foil to keep warm.

Wipe out the frying pan and return to medium heat. Add the remaining oil, the mushrooms and softened onion. Cook for 3 minutes, then add 250 ml (9 fl oz/1 cup) of cold water and the thyme and season with salt. Cook for 4 minutes or until the mushrooms have softened. Return the livers to the pan, reduce the heat to low and cook for 2 minutes or until the sauce has reduced by half. Turn the livers in the sauce. Cook for another 3 minutes. At this stage the livers should be pink in the centre and the sauce thick and sticky. Add the parsley and remove from the heat. Check the seasoning.

To serve, place the bottom halves of the ensaimadas on individual serving plates. Spoon the liver mixture and some of the sauce from the pan over the top. Place the top halves of the ensaimadas on top and serve straight away.

POTATO & BACON TERRINE WITH SMOKED EEL

10-12 RACIONES

TERRINA DE PATATA Y BACON CON ANGUILA AHUMADA

POTATO AND BACON TERRINE

1 KG (2 LB 4 OZ) WHITE-SKINNED POTATOES, WASHED AND PEELED

1 X 800 G (1 LB 12 OZ) SMOKED EEL (50-60 CM/20-24 INCHES LONG) (SEE NOTES)

100 G (3½ OZ) UNSALTED BUTTER, MELTED

1 TABLESPOON FINE SEA SALT

1 TABLESPOON FRESHLY GROUND BLACK PEPPER

100 G (3½ OZ) QUESO DE MANCHEGO (SEE GLOSSARY), FINELY GRATED

200 G (7 OZ) PIECE OF MIDDLE BACON, SLICED ACROSS THE GRAIN INTO 2 MM (⅟₁₆ INCH) THICK SLICES (SEE NOTES)

100 G (3½ OZ) RICE FLOUR

OLIVE OIL, FOR COOKING

30 G (1 OZ) FRESH HORSERADISH ROOT

SEA SALT FLAKES, FOR GARNISHING

PEA SALAD

500 G (1 LB 2 OZ) PODDED GREEN PEAS

200 G (7 OZ) SNOW PEA (MANGETOUT) TENDRILS

2½ TABLESPOONS CHARDONNAY VINEGAR

100 ML (3½ FL OZ) EXTRA VIRGIN OLIVE OIL, PLUS EXTRA FOR COOKING

This is one of our classic dishes that customers insist we keep on the menu. I was astounded to learn that eels have been smoked in Victoria by Aborigines for thousands of years. We're lucky to have an industry here that still harvests eels from the wild.

To make the potato and bacon terrine, thinly slice the potatoes into 2 mm (⅟₁₆ inch) thick rounds, using a mandolin or sharp knife. Cover and set aside.

Using your fingers, peel the skin from the eel and discard; it will come away easily. Remove and discard the bones, keeping the flesh intact. Using a sharp knife, cut the eel into 30 cm x 4 cm x 5 mm (12 inch x 1½ inch x ¼ inch) pieces.

Lightly grease a 30 cm x 8 cm (12 inch x 3¼ inch) terrine mould and line with a double layer of plastic wrap with enough overhang on the long sides to cover the mould. Brush the base with a little melted butter and carefully line with a neat layer of potato. As the potatoes at the base of the terrine will end up being on top when it's served, take a little time to attractively arrange the slices. Brush with a little more butter and sprinkle with a little fine sea salt, pepper and Manchego. Ensure you brush and sprinkle between each layer as you continue with the following instructions: add 2 layers of potato, then lay across one-third of the bacon. Add another 2 layers of potato. Add one-third of the eel. Continue this layering process making sure the double layer of potato sits between the eel and bacon otherwise the terrine won't set properly. Finish with 3 layers of potato. Brush with butter and season but don't sprinkle any cheese over the top layer. Fold the overhanging plastic wrap over the top of the potatoes to cover the terrine.

Preheat the oven to 160°C (315°F/Gas 2-3). Place the terrine in a roasting tray just slightly larger than the terrine. Place in the oven and fill the tray with hot water to come one-third of the way up the sides of the terrine. Bake for 1 hour 45 minutes. To test if the terrine is ready, insert a skewer into the terrine; if it meets very little resistance, then it's ready. Otherwise, cook for another 5-10 minutes.

Remove the terrine from the water bath. Cut out a piece of thick cardboard to fit inside the top of the terrine and wrap in foil. Place on top of the terrine, weigh it down with food cans and refrigerate overnight.

The next day, make the pea salad. Bring a saucepan of heavily salted water to the boil over high heat. Blanch the peas for 3 minutes. Drain and refresh in iced water. Drain again and gently crush the peas with the flat blade of a knife. Combine with the snow pea tendrils and set aside.

Combine the vinegar and olive oil in a bowl and season with salt and pepper to make a dressing and set aside.

Remove the terrine from the mould and peel off the plastic wrap. Slice into 2.5 cm (1 inch) thick slices using a sharp knife. Lightly dust both sides of the terrine slices with rice flour. Heat a 5 mm (¼ inch) layer of oil in a frying pan over medium-high heat and shallow-fry the terrine, in batches, for 3 minutes each side or until lightly golden and heated through. Drain on paper towel.

To serve, place a slice of terrine on each plate, place a small handful of pea salad on the side and spoon over a little dressing. Grate some horseradish over the terrine, sprinkle with sea salt and serve straight away.

NOTES: Smoked eel is available from select fishmongers and delicatessens, particularly Eastern European ones.

It is best to use a meat slicer to thinly slice the bacon. Ask your butcher to do this for you.

SALMON & POTATO TERRINE WITH BABY BEETROOT

10 RACIONES

TERRINA DE SALMÓN

SALMON & POTATO TERRINE

700 G (1 LB 9 OZ) WAXY POTATOES, SUCH AS
NICOLA OR ROYAL BLUE

250 G (9 OZ) GHEE OR CLARIFIED BUTTER
(SEE NOTE)

1 X 1 KG (2 LB 4 OZ) PIECE OF SKINLESS
SALMON FILLET

3 LARGE LEEKS

SEA SALT FLAKES

EXTRA VIRGIN OLIVE OIL, FOR DRIZZLING

30 G (1 OZ) FRESH HORSERADISH ROOT

BABY BEETROOT SALAD

30 BABY BEETROOTS (BEETS)

60 ML (2 FL OZ/¼ CUP) EXTRA VIRGIN OLIVE OIL,
PLUS EXTRA FOR COOKING

1 TABLESPOON CHARDONNAY VINEGAR

¼ CUP PARSLEY, FINELY CHOPPED

This is a serious restaurant dish. This book is a document of what we are doing at MoVida and sometimes restaurant food can't be replicated in a domestic kitchen without professional equipment. We're giving the recipe up but know that some of you won't ever make it... And then there are some of you who will.

You will need to begin this recipe the day before.

To make the salmon and potato terrine, peel and slice the potatoes into 5 mm (¼ inch) thick rounds. Heat the ghee in 2 x 24 cm (9½ inch) non-stick frying pans over low heat and cook the potato, turning occasionally, for 20 minutes or until tender but not browned. Drain on paper towel and set aside to cool.

Meanwhile, run your fingers over the piece of salmon and, using a pair of fish tweezers, remove all the protruding bones. Dip the tweezers into a small bowl of water to get the bones off. Pat the salmon dry with paper towel. Cut the salmon in half lengthways, then cut each piece in half crossways. Slice each piece into 2 fillets crossways. You should end up with 8 pieces about 2.5 cm (1 inch) thick. Set aside.

Trim and discard the green part from the leeks. Slightly trim the roots, keeping the base intact which will help keep the leeks together while they cook. Rinse the leeks to remove any grit. Bring a large saucepan of salted water to the boil over high heat. Blanch the leeks for 10 minutes or until just tender when pierced through with the tip of a knife. Drain and refresh in iced water. Drain again. Cut the leeks in half lengthways. Remove and discard the first few outside layers and separate the rest of the layers.

Lightly grease a 33 cm x 11 cm x 10 cm (13 inch x 4¼ inch x 4 inch) terrine mould and line with a double layer of plastic wrap with enough overhang on the long sides to cover the mould. Line the mould crossways with strips of leek, overlapping each piece neatly (as this will be the presentation side when serving). The ends of the strips should overhang over the edge almost to the bench. Line the mould with strips of leek lengthways in a similar manner. Patch the corners with a few extra strips, trimmed to fit. Cover the leeks with a layer of slightly overlapping potatoes. Season with salt. Arrange the salmon over the potatoes in a single layer with the cut sides sitting flush together, ensuring there are no gaps — you may need to trim some pieces to fit. Drizzle with a little olive oil, finely grate over some horseradish and season with salt. Cover the salmon with the remaining potato and season with salt. Fold the overhanging leek strips over the top to cover the potato and fold the overhanging plastic back over to cover. Lay a long, double layer of plastic wrap on a bench and carefully invert the terrine onto it. Lift off the mould and wrap the terrine tightly in the plastic wrap, then place back in the mould and refrigerate for 2 hours.

Carefully remove the terrine from the mould, place in a large high-density plastic bag. Follow our steps on sous-vide cooking (see page 123). Vacuum seal the bag, then place back in the mould. Place in a water bath and cook at 38°C (100°F) for 1¼ hours. Remove the bag from the water bath and place in iced water for 5 minutes. Remove the bag from the iced water and refrigerate overnight.

The next day, make the baby beetroot salad. Preheat the oven to 180°C (350°F/ Gas 4). Trim the beetroot stalks and discard. Wash the beetroot well. Place in a roasting tray, drizzle with the extra olive oil and roast for 25 minutes. Remove from the tray. Reserve any cooking juices.

Place the vinegar, oil, parsley and a few tablespoons of the reserved cooking juices in a small bowl and mix well to make a dressing.

When the beetroot are cool enough to handle, peel, then cut any large ones into halves or quarters. Leave to cool to room temperature.

To serve, place the terrine on a chopping board and remove the plastic wrap. Cut the terrine into 10 slices and place on individual serving plates. Spoon some beetroot salad onto the plate and garnish with sea salt.

NOTE: To make clarified butter, gently melt 300 g (10½ oz) of butter in a small saucepan over low heat. Remove from the heat and allow to stand for a few minutes for the milk solids to sink to the bottom. Pour the clear butterfat off the top and discard the milk solids. Clarified butter has a higher burning point and will keep refrigerated for 2 months.

DUCK LIVER PARFAIT WITH PEDRO XIMÉNEZ FOAM

8 RACIONES

PATÉ DE PATO

PEDRO XIMÉNEZ FOAM

350 ML (12 FL OZ) PEDRO XIMÉNEZ
SHERRY (SEE GLOSSARY)

4 X 2 G (¹⁄₁₆ OZ) GELATINE SHEETS
(GOLD STRENGTH)

1 EGG WHITE

DUCK LIVER PARFAIT

1 TABLESPOON EXTRA VIRGIN OLIVE OIL

½ BROWN ONION, SLICED

2 GARLIC CLOVES, SLICED

1 BAY LEAF

1 SPRIG THYME

1 TEASPOON FRESHLY GROUND BLACK PEPPER

2½ TEASPOONS FINE SEA SALT

125 ML (4 FL OZ/½ CUP) BRANDY

125 ML (4 FL OZ/½ CUP) FINO SHERRY
(SEE GLOSSARY)

125 ML (4 FL OZ/½ CUP) PEDRO XIMÉNEZ
SHERRY (SEE GLOSSARY)

600 G (1 LB 5 OZ) DUCK LIVERS, CLEANED
(SEE NOTE)

4 EGGS

500 G (1 LB 2 OZ) UNSALTED BUTTER, CUBED
AND AT ROOM TEMPERATURE

TO SERVE

8 X 5 MM (¼ INCH) THICK SLICES BRIOCHE
(SEE PAGE 13)

BLACK SEA SALT

Take a wonderfully rich duck liver parfait, make a foam with sweet Pedro Ximénez sherry and arrange it beautifully with squares of toasted brioche. We've served all these elements before at MoVida but it took Chef Robbo's signature touch of symmetry to take it this level.

You will need to begin this recipe the day before.

To make the Pedro Ximénez foam, place the sherry in a saucepan over medium heat and simmer rapidly for 3–4 minutes or until reduced to 300 ml (10½ fl oz). Remove from the heat and allow to cool slightly. Soak the gelatine sheets in cold water for about 2 minutes or until softened. Squeeze out the excess water, then add to the reduced sherry. Stir until the gelatine has dissolved, then pour into a bowl. Place the bowl on a bed of ice that comes at least halfway up the side of the bowl. Using hand-held electric beaters, beat the mixture on high speed for 4 minutes. At this point the mixture will have cooled down enough to start aerating. Add the egg white, which will help the mixture to aerate even more. Continue beating for 4 minutes, then pour into a lightly greased 20 cm x 16 cm x 4 cm (8 inch x 6¼ inch x 1½ inch) tray. Cover with plastic wrap and refrigerate overnight.

Meanwhile, make the duck liver parfait, heat the olive oil in a small heavy-based saucepan over medium–low heat. Cook the onion, garlic, bay leaf, thyme and black pepper for 15 minutes, stirring occasionally, or until the onion is soft. Add the salt, brandy and both sherries, increase the heat to high and bring to the boil, then reduce the heat to medium–low and simmer for 10 minutes or until the liquid has reduced by two-thirds and is thick and sticky. Remove the bay leaf and thyme. Allow to cool to room temperature.

Transfer the onion mixture to a blender. Add the livers and eggs and blend for 5 minutes or until smooth. Add the butter and blend for 5 minutes or until smooth. The mixture may split initially but it will come back together. Strain through a fine sieve placed over a bowl. Set aside.

Preheat the oven to 160°C (315°F/Gas 2–3). Lightly grease a 25 cm x 5 cm x 5 cm (10 inch x 2 inch x 2 inch) cast-iron terrine mould that has a lid and line with a double layer of plastic wrap with enough overhang on the long sides to cover the terrine. Pour the strained mixture into the mould and fold the plastic wrap over to cover. Cover with the lid and place in a roasting tray. Place in the oven and fill the tray with enough hot water to come three-quarters of the way up the sides of the terrine. Bake for 45–60 minutes or until set and the internal temperature of the parfait reaches 69°C (156°F). Remove the terrine from the water bath and allow to cool slightly before refrigerating for at least 3 hours or overnight.

The next day, neatly trim the crusts from the slices of brioche and toast until lightly golden. Cut each slice into neat 4 cm (1½ inch) squares.

Remove the parfait from the mould and place on a chopping board. Using a sharp knife dipped in hot water, cut into 18 neat 4 cm (1½ inch) cubes, wiping the knife between slices to ensure the edges are as smooth as possible. If the sides look a little rough, smooth over with a small palette knife or spatula.

Remove the foam from the mould and place on a chopping board. Using a sharp knife dipped in hot water, cut into neat 4 cm (1¼ inch) cubes.

To serve, place 2 parfait cubes onto each serving plate. Arrange a foam cube alongside with 8 squares of brioche. Garnish with black salt.

NOTE: You will need 500 g (1 lb 2 oz) cleaned duck liver.

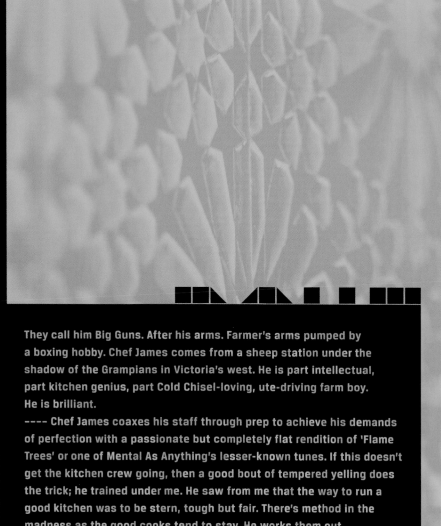

They call him Big Guns. After his arms. Farmer's arms pumped by
a boxing hobby. Chef James comes from a sheep station under the
shadow of the Grampians in Victoria's west. He is part intellectual,
part kitchen genius, part Cold Chisel-loving, ute-driving farm boy.
He is brilliant.

---- Chef James coaxes his staff through prep to achieve his demands
of perfection with a passionate but completely flat rendition of 'Flame
Trees' or one of Mental As Anything's lesser-known tunes. If this doesn't
get the kitchen crew going, then a good bout of tempered yelling does
the trick; he trained under me. He saw from me that the way to run a
good kitchen was to be stern, tough but fair. There's method in the
madness as the good cooks tend to stay. He works them out.

---- What goes onto the plate from his kitchen at Aqui is a mix of
exuberant Phil Spector style wall of flavour such as wild barramundi
wrapped in fresh wakame served on a bed of Jerusalem artichoke and
truffle purée with a fino-sherry-based sauce. Or it could be a quietly
restrained Catalan-inspired dish of slices of raw tomato, shreds of
bacalao (salt cod) and a few marjoram leaves and arbequina olive
oil. He simply gets Spanish food. He follows the way we use whole
carcasses, make sausages, morcilla and chorizo. Nothing gets
wasted — any off-cuts are turned into an aspect of another dish.

---- I think of Chef James as a Merino — a truly Spanish beast
making its home in Australia. Then again I don't think any Spaniard
has ever sung so tunelessly. As Mental's Martin Plaza sang,
"Try not to break me baby you're so strong."

BRINED LAMB SHOULDER WITH SAFFRON POTATOES

6 RACIONES

CORDERO AL HORNO

BRINED LAMB

200 G (7 OZ) COOKING SALT

2 TABLESPOONS BLACK PEPPERCORNS

PEEL OF 1 ORANGE

PEEL OF 1 LEMON

2 CINNAMON STICKS

2 STAR ANISE

3 BAY LEAVES

2 SPRIGS MARJORAM

1.8 KG (4 LB) LAMB FOREQUARTER LEG, BONE IN

80 ML (2½ FL OZ/⅓ CUP) EXTRA VIRGIN OLIVE OIL

1 TEASPOON SEA SALT

SAUCE

1 KG (2 LB 4 OZ) VEAL BONES

2 TABLESPOONS VEGETABLE OIL

2 CARROTS, CUT INTO LARGE PIECES

2 BROWN ONIONS, CUT INTO LARGE PIECES

2 TABLESPOONS TOMATO PASTE (CONCENTRATED PURÉE)

100 ML (3½ FL OZ) RED WINE

1½ TABLESPOONS CABERNET SAUVIGNON VINEGAR

1 TEASPOON LEMON JUICE

2 SPRIGS MINT

SAFFRON POTATOES

2½ TABLESPOONS EXTRA VIRGIN OLIVE OIL

2 BROWN ONIONS, SLICED

½ TEASPOON SAFFRON THREADS

1 TABLESPOON DRIED OREGANO

4 LARGE WAXY POTATOES, CUT INTO 3 CM (1¼ INCH) CUBES

SEA SALT AND FRESHLY GROUND BLACK PEPPER

200 ML (7 FL OZ) FINO SHERRY

4 GARLIC CLOVES, THINLY SLICED

Take the forequarter leg of lamb and brine it in an aromatic solution with the classic Spanish combination of cinnamon and citrus, slowly cook it in a water bath, then finish it off on a bed of saffron potatoes drizzled with infused red wine jus. God it's good.

You will need to begin this recipe 2 days ahead.

To make the brined lamb, combine the cooking salt, peppercorns, citrus peel, spices and herbs, in a large saucepan with 2 litres (70 fl oz) of water, bring to the boil, then reduce the heat to a simmer and cook for 5 minutes to infuse. Allow to cool completely.

Add the lamb to the cooled brine, cover and refrigerate for 24 hours.

The next day, remove the lamb from the brine and place in a large high-density plastic bag. Follow our steps on sous-vide cooking (see page 123). Vacuum seal the bags and cook in a water bath at 70°C (158°F) for 24 hours. Remove the bag from the water bath and place in iced water. You can refrigerate the lamb for up to 4 days. The lamb should be very tender at this stage. Alternatively, you can slow cook the lamb in a preheated 140°C (275°F/Gas 1) oven for 5 hours.

The next day, make the sauce. Preheat the oven to 180°C (350°F/Gas 4). Spread the veal bones over a large baking tray and roast for 40 minutes.

Heat the vegetable oil in a heavy-based stockpot over high heat and cook the carrot and onion for about 15 minutes until really well browned, almost black. Add the tomato paste and cook, stirring continuously, for a further 10 minutes. Deglaze with the wine, scraping any cooked-on bits from the base of the pot.

Add the roasted bones, cover with 1.3 litres (44 fl oz) of water, bring to the boil, then reduce the heat to low and simmer for 3 hours or until reduced by one-third, skimming the surface regularly to remove any impurities.

Strain the stock into a clean wide-based saucepan and discard the solids. Place over high heat and reduce the stock to about 100 ml (3½ fl oz).

Add the vinegar, lemon juice and mint and bring back to the boil, then reduce heat to low and simmer for a further 10 minutes. Strain again and check the seasoning. Transfer to a pouring jug and keep warm until ready to serve. Refrigerate if not using immediately and reheat gently to serve.

To make the saffron potatoes, heat the olive oil in a large heavy-based saucepan over medium–low heat. Add the onion, saffron and dried oregano, cover and gently cook, stirring occasionally, for 15–20 minutes or until softened. Add the potato and season with salt and pepper. Add the sherry, garlic and 300 ml (10½ fl oz) of water, cover and cook for 30 minutes or until the potato is tender. Transfer to a 36 cm x 22 cm (14¼ inch x 8½ inch) oval terracotta baking dish or similar vessel.

To serve, preheat the oven to 220°C (425°F/Gas 7). Remove the lamb from the plastic bag, discarding any of the juices from the bag. Place the lamb on top of the potato, drizzle with the olive oil, season with the sea salt and rub in. Roast for 40 minutes or until golden, turning the lamb halfway through the cooking time. Allow to rest on top of the potaoes, then carve at the table. Pour over some of the warm sauce to serve.

MoVida is so much more than about any one individual. It is about how we all work together. For years, Chef James and I scrambled every day to come up with desserts. I do so love a sweet ending to a meal but I don't have a naturally occurring sweet tooth. I was born with a fat tooth. I love my butter and cream. Luckily the rest of my chefs balance that out. Here's a selection of desserts that reflect the casual way of dining we love. Some are petite, some are no more than a few mouthfuls and some are served in a glass, which means you don't have to stop at one spoonful.

POSTRES

DESSERTS

SLOE BRANDY & CONSERVED PEACHES

SERVES 6

PACHARÁN AL MELOCTON

850 G (1 LB 14 OZ) GOOD-QUALITY PEACHES PRESERVED IN SUGAR SYRUP

330 ML (11¼ OZ/1⅓ CUPS) PACHARÁN (SEE NOTE)

2½ TABLESPOONS LEMON JUICE

SEASONAL FRUIT OF YOUR CHOICE

At the end of a meal in Spain, a waiter may bring you a powerful little shot of alcohol, on the house, to cut through all the food you've just consumed. In the Basque country, they serve a wickedly powerful brandy, made with sloe berries, called pacharán (or patxaran). It's so powerful, we've tempered it with conserved peaches from our own garden to give a slightly less blatant alcoholic end to the evening.

Drain the peaches and reserve 75 ml (2⅔ fl oz) of the sugar syrup. Place the peaches, pacharán and lemon juice in a food processor and process for a few minutes or until the mixture becomes a smooth purée. Transfer to a container and refrigerate until chilled.

Peel, if necessary, and dice the seasonal fruit into 2 cm (¾ inch) cubes. If using melons, use a melon baller to scoop out small balls of fruit. Thread 3 pieces of fruit onto a skewer. Repeat to make 6 skewers and refrigerate until chilled.

To serve, chill 6 x 100 ml (3½ fl oz) glasses. Pour the peach purée into each glass and garnish with a fruit skewer. Serve straight away.

NOTE: Pacharán is available from good-quality liquor stores.

244

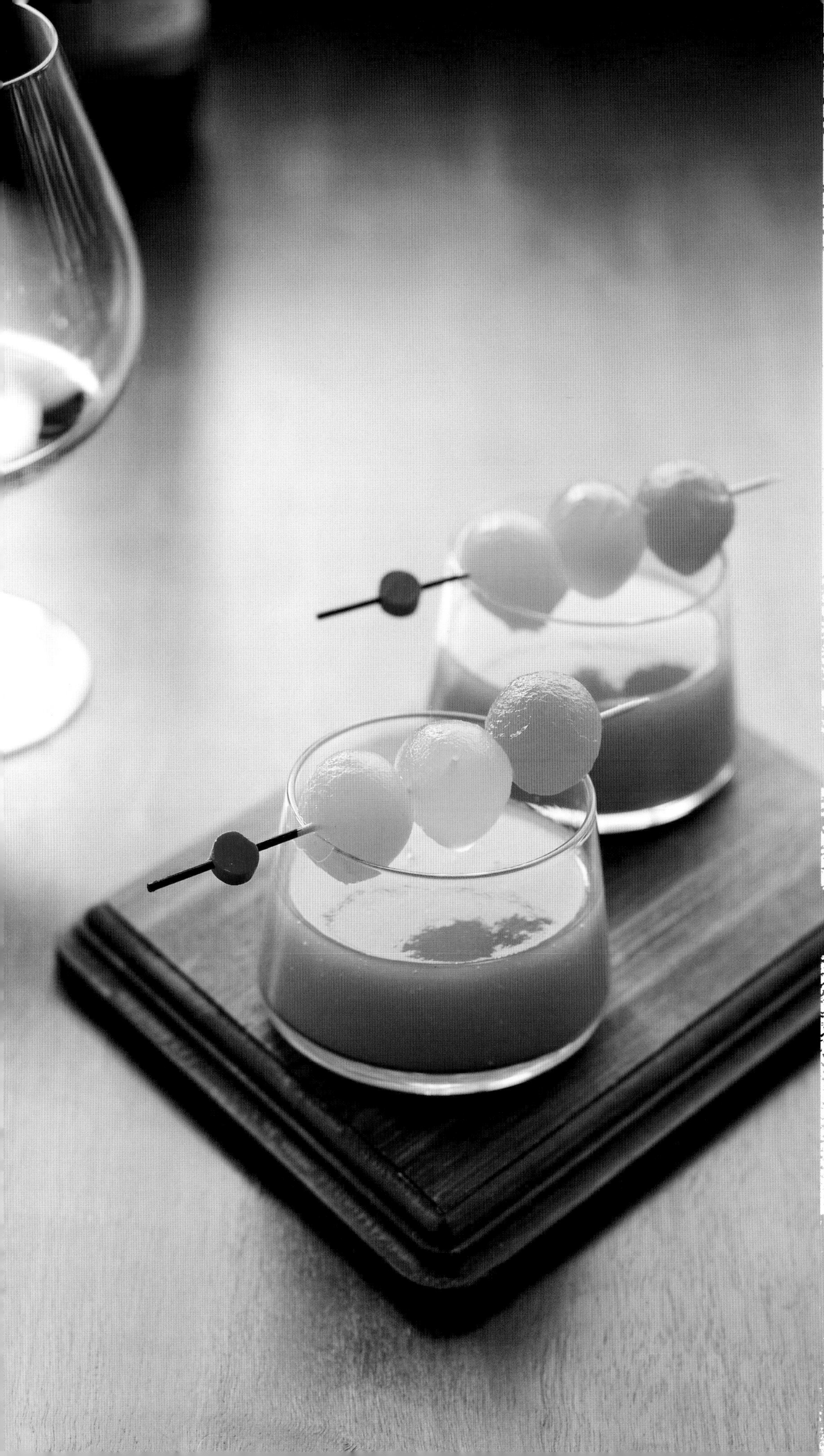

COFFEE & RUM GRANITA WITH CRÈME CATALAN FOAM

SERVES 8

GRANISADO DEL CARAJILLO CON CREMA CATALANA

RUM TRUFFLES

270 ML (9½ FL OZ) POURING (SINGLE) CREAM

50 G (1¾ OZ) LIQUID GLUCOSE

380 G (13½ OZ) VALRHONA DARK CHOCOLATE
  (64% COCOA SOLIDS)

40 ML (1¼ FL OZ) DARK RUM

GOOD-QUALITY COCOA POWDER, FOR DUSTING

COFFEE & RUM GRANITA

250 ML (9 FL OZ/1 CUP) HOT ESPRESSO
  COFFEE

125 G (4½ OZ) CASTER (SUPERFINE) SUGAR

100 ML (3½ FL OZ) DARK RUM

250 ML (9 FL OZ/1 CUP) SPARKLING MINERAL
  WATER

CREMA CATALANA FOAM

1 QUANTITY CREMA CATALANA
  (SEE PAGES 260-1)

TO SERVE

GROUND CINNAMON, FOR DUSTING

I like to think that this is the tapa of the dessert world. Carajillo is a coffee laced with brandy, anis liqueur or rum. When you order carajillo in Spain, the bartender will warm a little lemon peel over a lighter and put it in the coffee. Despite the dark rum and rich crema, because it is such a petite serve, you don't have to stop at just one dessert. You can order a second or third dessert and feel none the worse for wear.

To make the rum truffles, place the cream and the liquid glucose in a small saucepan over medium heat, stirring to dissolve the glucose. Increase the heat to high and bring just to the boil. Remove from the heat and allow to cool to 50°C–60°C (122°F–140°F).

Place the chocolate in the top of a double boiler over medium heat or in a heatproof bowl in a hot water bath (do not allow any water into the chocolate or it will become grainy) and stir until melted and smooth. Combine with the warm cream. Add the rum and mix well.

Pour the mixture into a shallow 18 cm x 10 cm (7 inch x 4 inch) tin lined with baking paper. Smooth the top and freeze for 6 hours.

Meanwhile, make the coffee and rum granita. Place the coffee and sugar in a large bowl and stir until the sugar has dissolved. Add the rum and mineral water. Pour into a shallow stainless steel 30 cm x 24 cm (12 inch x 9½ inch) tray and place in the freezer. Scrape with a fork every 30 minutes for a few hours or until frozen with even ice-crystal formation.

Remove the frozen rum truffle slab from the freezer. Using a knife dipped in hot water, cut the slab into 2 cm (¾ inch) squares. Spread the cocoa powder on a plate and roll the truffles in the cocoa until well coated. Place on a tray lined with baking paper and refrigerate for 1 hour or until firm. This makes more truffles than you will need (see notes).

Meanwhile, make the crema catalana foam. Set aside to cool for 1 hour, then pour the crema catalana into a cream canister and charge with 2 soda bulbs (see glossary). Shake well. This makes more crema catalana than you will need (see notes).

To serve, chill 8 small glasses (about 5 cm/2 inches in diameter and 8 cm/3¼ inches deep). Fill the glasses one-third with the granita. Spray the crema catalana over the granita, filling the glasses to the top. Dust with a little cinnamon and place 2 truffles to one side.

NOTES: Store extra truffles in an airtight container in the fridge for up to 7 days.
Store the excess crema catalana in the cream canister in the fridge for up to 3 days.

PINEAPPLE GAZPACHO WITH PONCHE SOTO GRANITA

SERVES 8

GAZPACHO DE PIÑA CON GRANISADO PONCHE SOTO

PINEAPPLE CRISPS

1 X 1.5 KG (3 LB 5 OZ) PINEAPPLE

200 G (7 OZ) CASTER (SUPERFINE) SUGAR

2 VANILLA BEANS

PINEAPPLE GAZPACHO

2 X 1.5 KG (3 LB 5 OZ) PINEAPPLES

400 G (14 OZ) CASTER (SUPERFINE) SUGAR

1 SMALL FRESH OLD COCONUT, CRACKED AND
  JUICE COLLECTED, GRATE 100 G (3½ OZ)
  OF THE COCONUT FLESH

PONCHE SOTO GRANITA

250 G (9 OZ) CASTER (SUPERFINE) SUGAR

½ BUNCH MINT

150 ML (5 FL OZ) PONCHE SOTO

150 ML (5 FL OZ) SPARKLING MINERAL WATER

TO SERVE

16 STRAWBERRIES, HULLED AND HALVED

120 G (4¼ OZ) RASPBERRIES

200 G (7 OZ) BLUEBERRIES

Gazpacho isn't just a cold vegetable soup. It can be a cold fruit soup as well, made with perhaps watermelon or cherries. Younger Spanish chefs are making these sweet fruit soups – ice cold, fresh and fruity, brilliantly refreshing. If you can't find Ponche Soto, a Spanish apéritif, use a sweet liqueur of your choice.

You will need to begin this recipe the day before.

To make the pineapple crisps, remove the skin from the pineapple and, using a serrated knife, thinly slice crossways into 2 mm (1/16 inch) thick rounds or as thin as possible. Place in a stainless steel bowl. Place 400 ml (14 fl oz) of water and the sugar in a saucepan over high heat, stirring until the sugar has dissolved, and bring to the boil. Cut the vanilla beans in half lengthways, add to the sugar syrup and continue to boil for 5 minutes. Allow to cool, then pour over the pineapple. Cover with plastic wrap and refrigerate overnight.

The next day, make the pineapple gazpacho. Remove the skin from the pineapples and remove the cores. Cut the pineapple flesh into small chunks and place in a stainless steel bowl. Place 1 litre (35 fl oz/4 cups) of water and the sugar in a saucepan over high heat, stirring until the sugar has dissolved, and bring to the boil. Pour over the pineapple, cover with plastic wrap and leave at room temperature for 8–10 hours.

Meanwhile, crack the coconut and tip out the coconut juice into a bowl. You will need 250 ml (9 fl oz/1 cup) of juice. Set aside. Cover the coconut with plastic wrap, refrigerate and reserve the flesh for serving.

To make the Ponche Soto granita, place 500 ml (17 fl oz/2 cups) of water and the sugar in a saucepan over high heat, stirring to dissolve the sugar, and bring to the boil. Add the mint and Ponche Soto, remove from the heat and allow to infuse for 15 minutes, then add the mineral water and allow to cool completely.

Pour into a shallow stainless steel 30 cm x 24 cm x (12 inch x 9½ inch) tray and place in the freezer. Scrape with a fork every 30 minutes for a few hours or until frozen with even ice-crystal formation.

Meanwhile, bake the pineapple crisps. Preheat the oven to 90°C (194°F). Remove the pineapple from the fridge and remove from the syrup. Lay flat on baking trays lined with baking paper. Place in the oven and leave to dry for 2–3 hours or until crisp.

Meanwhile, blend the pineapple gazpacho. Drain the pineapple in a sieve placed over a bowl, reserving the juice. Place the pineapple in a food processor and process with enough of the reserved juice to achieve the same consistency as pouring custard. Transfer to a non-reactive bowl, stir in the reserved coconut juice, cover with plastic wrap and refrigerate until ready to use.

To serve, chill 8 x 250 ml (9 fl oz/1 cup) capacity tumblers. Using a coconut scraper, scrape the reserved coconut flesh so you have about 100 g (3½ oz) grated coconut.

Spoon about 150 ml (5 fl oz) of the gazpacho into each tumbler, then divide the berries between the glasses. Top each with 2 heaped tablespoons of granita and scatter over a little grated coconut. Garnish with the pineapple crisps.

BAKED CHEESECAKE WITH RHUBARB & ALMOND

SERVES 6

TARTA DE QUESO

BAKED CHEESECAKE

300 G (10½ OZ) SHEEP'S MILK CURD
 (SEE NOTES)

35 G (1¼ OZ) CASTER (SUPERFINE) SUGAR

20 G (¾ OZ) SOFT BROWN SUGAR

FINELY GRATED ZEST AND JUICE OF 1 LEMON

2 EGGS

1 EGG YOLK

ALMOND CRUNCH

200 G (7 OZ/2 CUPS) GROUND ALMONDS
 (ALMOND MEAL)

40 G (1½ OZ) SOFT BROWN SUGAR

50 G (1¾ OZ) UNSALTED BUTTER

GLAZED RHUBARB

1 STALK RHUBARB

50 ML (1¾ FL OZ) LICOR 43 (SEE NOTES)

30 G (1 OZ) CASTER (SUPERFINE) SUGAR

Chef Robbo took the cheesecake I was shown how to cook by a Basque chef and made it pretty. The original was undeniably delicious but had a blackened crust only a mother could love. Robbo made it small and made it beautiful.

To make the baked cheesecake, preheat the oven to 110°C (225°F/Gas ½). Lightly grease 6 x 7 cm (2¾ inch) diameter x 4 cm (1½ inch) deep stainless steel ring moulds. Wrap one side of each ring with a square of aluminium foil and secure with an elastic band to form a base. Place the moulds, foil-side down, in a deep baking dish.

Place the sheep's milk curd, both sugars, lemon juice and zest, eggs and egg yolk in a blender and blend for 1 minute or just until combined and smooth — do not over-blend or you will incorporate air into the mixture. Pour the mixture into the prepared moulds. Place the baking dish in the oven and fill it with enough hot water to come halfway up the sides of the moulds. Bake for 40 minutes or until just beginning to set. To test if they're ready, give the moulds a little shake; they should be dry to the touch but still wobble. Remove from the oven and carefully remove from the water bath. Allow to cool completely and firm up.

Next, make the almond crunch. Increase the oven temperature to 150°C (300°F/Gas 2). Place the ground almonds, sugar and butter in a saucepan over low heat and cook until the butter has melted. Spread over a baking tray lined with baking paper. Bake for 15 minutes or until golden. Allow to cool on the tray, then break into finger-nail-sized pieces.

Meanwhile, make the glazed rhubarb. Peel the rhubarb and cut into 1 cm (½ inch) lengths. Place the Licor 43, sugar and 100 ml (3½ fl oz) of water in a small saucepan over medium heat, stirring until the sugar dissolves. Bring to the boil, then add the rhubarb and cook for 4 minutes or until soft. Remove the rhubarb with a slotted spoon and set aside. Continue to cook the liquid for 6 minutes or until reduced by two-thirds to a thick glaze. Remove from the heat and return the rhubarb to the pan.

To serve, remove the cheesecakes from their rings. Peel off the foil from each, run a knife around the inside rim of the mould and gently slide the cheesecake out and place on individual serving plates. Spoon around a few pieces of glazed rhubarb and a little of the glaze and finish with some of the almond crunch. If you like, briefly caramelise the tops of the cheesecakes with a kitchen blowtorch.

NOTES: You can also use goat's milk curd. You can find both at select supermarkets, delicatessens and health food stores.

Licor 43 is a bright yellow Spanish liqueur made from 43 different aromatic ingredients and has a vanilla–citrus flavour. It's available from bottle shops specialising in Spanish drinks.

RICE PUDDING & CARAJILLO ICE-CREAM

SERVES 6

ARROZ CON LECHE

CARAJILLO ICE-CREAM

- 2 ORANGES
- 1 LEMON
- 1 CINNAMON STICK
- 1 LITRE (35 FL OZ/4 CUPS) POURING (SINGLE) CREAM
- 8 EGG YOLKS
- 200 G (7 OZ) CASTER (SUPERFINE) SUGAR
- 100 ML (3½ FL OZ) FRESHLY MADE ESPRESSO COFFEE
- 90 ML (3 FL OZ) BRANDY

RICE PUDDING

- 2 ORANGES
- 2 LEMONS
- 2 LITRES (70 FL OZ) MILK
- 370 G (13 OZ) CASTER (SUPERFINE) SUGAR
- 3 CINNAMON STICKS
- 200 G (7 OZ) BOMBA RICE (SEE GLOSSARY)
- 80 G (2¾ OZ) VALRHONA DARK CHOCOLATE (70% COCOA SOLIDS), CHOPPED
- 30 G (1 OZ) UNSALTED BUTTER
- 80 ML (2½ FL OZ/⅓ CUP) POURING (SINGLE) CREAM

We really wanted a heart-warming winter dessert in this book and this is it, the Spanish classic of rice pudding topped with a little chocolate sauce.

To make the carajillo ice-cream, using a small knife or vegetable peeler, remove the peel of the oranges and lemon in large, thin pieces, avoiding the white pith. Place in a saucepan with the cinnamon and cream and bring to the boil over medium heat. Remove from the heat and allow to infuse for 5 minutes, then remove the flavourings.

Lightly whisk the egg yolks and sugar together in a large bowl. Gradually add the warm cream mixture, a little at a time, gently stirring until well combined and smooth. Pour into a clean pan over medium–low heat and cook, stirring regularly, for 10 minutes or until the mixture reaches 82°C (180°F) and coats the back of a spoon. Stir in the espresso and brandy, remove from the heat and cool slightly. Strain through a fine sieve, then cover with plastic wrap touching the surface and refrigerate for 2 hours or until chilled. Pour into an ice-cream maker and churn according to the manufacturer's instructions. Place in the freezer until ready to use.

To make the rice pudding, using a small knife or vegetable peeler, remove the peel of the oranges and lemon in large, thin pieces, avoiding the white pith. Place in a large heavy-based saucepan with the milk, sugar and cinnamon over medium heat and bring just to a simmer. Sprinkle in the rice, reduce the heat to as low as possible so it is a bare simmer (use a heat diffuser, if necessary) and cook, stirring regularly, for 1 hour or until the rice is tender and has absorbed most of the liquid.

Towards the end of the cooking time, place the chocolate, butter and cream in a small heavy-based saucepan over very low heat and stir until just melted and combined. Remove from the heat and cover to keep warm. Pour the rice pudding into a large deep tray. This will make it easy to find and remove every last piece of citrus peel and the cinnamon sticks with tongs.

To serve, spoon the rice pudding into warmed serving dishes. Make an indentation in the rice with the back of a spoon and fill with a couple of spoonfuls of chocolate sauce. Top with a scoop of the ice-cream.

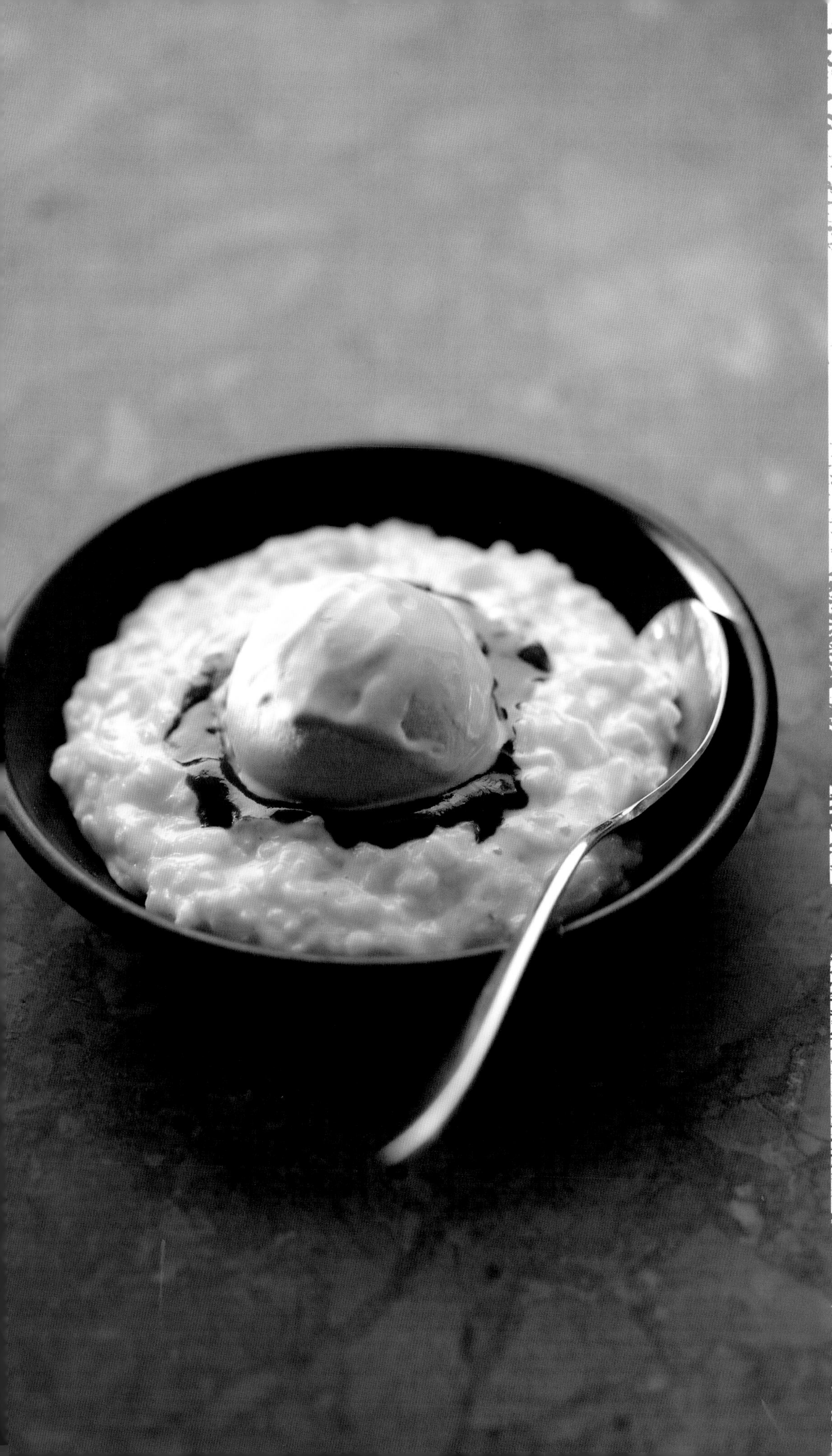

TRIFLE

SERVES 6

CREMA
INGLESA

SPONGE

125 G (4½ OZ) CASTER (SUPERFINE) SUGAR

1 VANILLA BEAN

4 EGGS

125 G (4½ OZ) PLAIN (ALL-PURPOSE) FLOUR

25 G (1 OZ) UNSALTED BUTTER, MELTED

CREMA CATALANA

500 ML (17 FL OZ/2 CUPS) POURING
    (SINGLE) CREAM

75 ML (2¾ FL OZ) MILK

FINELY GRATED ZEST OF 1 LEMON

FINELY GRATED ZEST OF 1 ORANGE

1 CINNAMON STICK

1 VANILLA BEAN

3 EGG YOLKS

60 G (2¼ OZ) CASTER (SUPERFINE) SUGAR

MACERATED STRAWBERRIES

500 G (1 LB 2 OZ) STRAWBERRIES

100 G (3½ OZ) CASTER (SUPERFINE) SUGAR

FINELY GRATED ZEST OF 1 ORANGE

FINELY GRATED ZEST AND JUICE OF 1 LEMON

1 VANILLA BEAN

SUGARED ALMONDS

155 G (5½ OZ) RAW ALMONDS

230 G (8 OZ) CASTER (SUPERFINE) SUGAR

PEDRO XIMÉNEZ JELLY

375 ML (13 FL OZ/½ CUPS) PEDRO XIMÉNEZ
    SHERRY (SEE GLOSSARY)

1 CINNAMON STICK

3 X 2 G (¹⁄₁₆ OZ) GELATINE SHEETS
    (GOLD STRENGTH)

Our pastry chef, Michael (see page 22), is English, so naturally the first dessert he made for us was a trifle. But it wasn't just any ordinary trifle. He had absorbed so much about Spanish pastry making and took what he had learned about using alcohol, fruit and custards that he turned the classic on its head. It was a magnificent Spanish crema inglesa made with crema catalana and Pedro Ximénez sherry. This is truly stunning.

You will need to begin this recipe the day before.

To make the sponge, preheat the oven to 160°C (315°F/Gas 2–3). Line a 28 cm x 22 cm (11¼ inch x 8½ inch) sponge roll tin with baking paper. Place the sugar in a bowl. Cut the vanilla bean in half lengthways and, using the tip of a knife, scrape the seeds into the bowl. Discard the vanilla bean (or reserve to make vanilla sugar).

Place the eggs in the bowl of an electric mixer with a balloon whisk attachment and whisk on medium speed for 1 minute. Increase the speed to high and slowly add the sugar mixture. Continue whisking for 8–10 minutes. At this point the sugar should have dissolved and the mixture will have tripled in volume. Transfer to a bowl.

Sift in the flour, add the melted butter and gently fold through using a spatula until incorporated. Pour into the prepared tin and bake for 15 minutes or until a skewer inserted into the centre comes out clean. Cool completely in the tin, then cover with plastic wrap and leave at room temperature overnight.

Meanwhile, make the crema catalana. Place the cream, milk, citrus zests and cinnamon in a heavy-based saucepan over medium heat. Cut the vanilla bean in half lengthways and, using the tip of a knife, scrape the seeds into the pan and add the bean, too. Bring to a simmer, then remove from the heat and allow to infuse for a few minutes. Strain into a bowl and discard the solids.

Lightly whisk the egg yolks and sugar together in a large bowl. Gradually add the warm cream mixture, a little at a time, gently stirring until well combined and smooth. Pour into a clean pan over medium–low heat and cook, stirring regularly, until the mixture reaches 82°C (180°F) or until it coats the back of a spoon. Strain into a bowl, cover with plastic wrap touching the surface and refrigerate overnight.

The next day, macerate the strawberries. Wash, hull and quarter the strawberries and place in a stainless steel bowl. Place the sugar, citrus zests, lemon juice and 100 ml (3½ fl oz) of water in a saucepan over medium heat. Cut the vanilla bean in half lengthways and, using the tip of a knife, scrape the seeds into the pan and add the bean, too. Bring to the boil, skimming off any impurities, then pour over the strawberries. Allow to macerate for 3 hours at room temperature.

Meanwhile, make the sugared almonds. Place the almonds, sugar and 250 ml (9 fl oz/1 cup) of water in a small heavy-based frying pan over medium–high heat and stir with a wooden spoon for 5–8 minutes or until the syrup begins to thicken. As the liquid becomes thicker and more viscous, the bubbles will become larger and appear more sluggish when they burst. Reduce the heat to medium–low and stir gently for 1 minute. The liquid will become white and frothy. Remove from the heat and allow just the very edge of the frying pan to remain in contact with the heat. Crystals will appear on the side of the pan — stir these into the mixture to hasten the crystallisation. Stir the mixture continuously until it begins to thicken again — you will feel more resistance as the crystals begin to form. Remove from the heat completely and continue mixing until it cools. Larger crystals will form around the almonds and the bits that do not stick to the almonds will have the appearance of breadcrumbs. Stir for another 2 minutes, then return to high heat. The sugar will begin to melt and some of it will start to caramelise. When there is a fine layer of caramel over some of the crystals, remove from the heat — do not allow more than one-fifth of the crystals to melt before removing. Pour onto a silicone baking mat or a baking tray lined with baking paper. Allow to cool completely.

About 45 minutes before serving, make the Pedro Ximénez jelly. Place the sherry and cinnamon in a small saucepan over medium heat and heat to 50°C (122°F). Remove from the heat and allow to infuse for 5 minutes. Remove and discard the cinnamon. Soak the gelatine sheets in cold water for 2 minutes or until softened. Squeeze out the excess water and whisk into the sherry mixture until dissolved. Allow to cool to room temperature. As it cools, it will thicken slightly.

To assemble, place 6 x 240 ml (8 fl oz) conical tumblers on a tray. Remove the sponge cake from its tin and place on a chopping board. Cut out circles from the sponge to fit the base of the glasses. Gently press the sponge into each glass. Spoon about 1 tablespoon of liquid from the macerated strawberries over each sponge, then cover with 4–5 teaspoons of macerated strawberries. Use the back of a spoon to push down a little to eliminate any air pockets. Top each with 3 tablespoons of the jelly and refrigerate for 30 minutes to allow the jelly to set.

To serve, spoon about 80 ml (2½ fl oz/⅓ cup) of the crema catalana into each glass and sprinkle with the sugared almonds. Serve straight away.

DRUNKEN APPLES WITH BLUE CHEESE

SERVES 4

MANZANAS BORRACHAS

2 GREEN APPLES, UNPEELED	200 G (7 OZ) QUESO DE VALDEÓN CHEESE
200 ML (7 FL OZ) MANZANILLA SHERRY	OR OTHER CREAMY FULL-FLAVOURED BLUE
(SEE GLOSSARY)	CHEESE, QUARTERED
100 ML (3½ FL OZ) SWEET APPLE LIQUEUR	TOASTED FRUIT BREAD, TO SERVE

You have to respect apples. They can soak up almost half their weight in alcohol and still look great. We prefer to use a clear Spanish apple liqueur but the French, English and Australians make a good version, too – just avoid the ones coloured an unnatural shade of bright green.

You will need to begin this recipe the day before.

Halve the apples, remove the cores and discard. Cut each half into 4–5 thin wedges. Place in a high-density plastic bag with the sherry and apple liqueur. Follow our steps on page 123 to vacuum seal the bag, then refrigerate for 24 hours.

The next day, 20 minutes before you're ready to serve, remove the apples from the fridge and set aside at room temperature.

To serve, place 4 apple wedges, a piece of cheese and the fruit bread on individual serving plates.

FRANK
LOOKING BACK

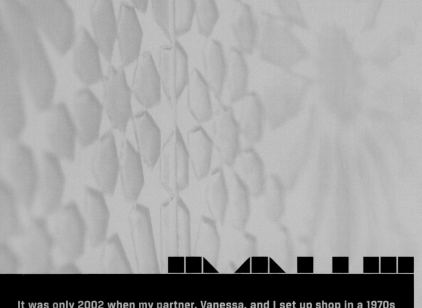

It was only 2002 when my partner, Vanessa, and I set up shop in a 1970s pub on the fringe of Melbourne. I had long finished my apprenticeship and had come back from a year cooking in Spanish kitchens. We started out serving the usual entrée-main-dessert formula. I was frightened people wouldn't get Spanish food; tapas had already earned a bad name after a series of poorly executed tapas bars in Melbourne during the 1990s. A top food consultant even told me I was mad to open a Spanish restaurant as no one liked the food. Our first guest was a vet. He came back with his son-in-law, a young man from Madrid. He looked up from his plate of morcilla and simply nodded and smiled. Trust me – Spanish people rarely compliment you. That was gold.

---- We trundled along for a while but we weren't setting the world on fire. We were busy and we were working the bar staff hard. Andy Mac, my business partner to this day, started back then with me with nothing more than a loose gentleman's agreement. He took the bar takings and I took the kitchen's. Back then he was a kid who had the hospitality experience of a teenager. Sure he had eaten in the best restaurants in the country but he still couldn't polish a glass – which was a bit of a worry as we were bringing in a new type of customer who was keeping him busy, the type of person who expected a new glass when they switched from white wine to red. Andy was funny but, more importantly, he could make people laugh with him, so we weren't too worried about him.

---- But something was wrong. Vanessa, a straight shooter, looked at me with her 'what the f**k are you doing?' eyes and said, "Just do what feels right. Don't try and meet other people's expectations". That was what I needed to hear. We tore up the menus and put on tapas and raciones and went for broke. We've never looked back. Andy Mac just kept on laughing and helped make everything we did fun. You can do that in a pub. You can stuff up a little bit and get away with it because it's just a pub. We had an absolute ball – and the ball has just kept rolling. That sense of relaxed fun is something we take everywhere with us. Life's too important to take seriously.

---- Finally I'd like to dedicate this book to Vanessa, Pepe and Hugo.

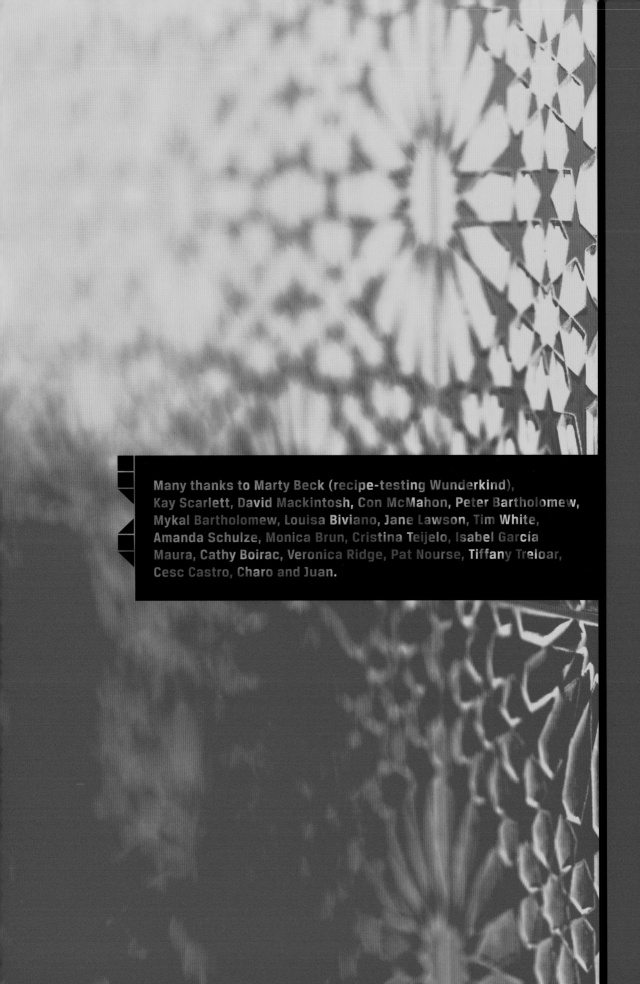

Many thanks to Marty Beck (recipe-testing Wunderkind),
Kay Scarlett, David Mackintosh, Con McMahon, Peter Bartholomew,
Mykal Bartholomew, Louisa Biviano, Jane Lawson, Tim White,
Amanda Schulze, Monica Brun, Cristina Teijelo, Isabel García
Maura, Cathy Boirac, Veronica Ridge, Pat Nourse, Tiffany Treloar,
Cesc Castro, Charo and Juan.

AGRADECIMIENTOS
ACKNOWLEDGEMENTS

GLOSSARY / GLOSARIO

Spanish food relies on a foundation of good ingredients. Some are indispensable and there are no alternatives. A little hunting around will be rewarded with delicious-tasting food.

ANCHOVIES

We love the wonderfully soft, deep rose coloured anchovies that are preserved at ports along the Cantabrian coast in the north of Spain. Left to mature in a super salty brine for eight months, they are then hand-filleted, packed in a little olive oil and shipped in refrigerated containers to keep their freshness.

BACALAO (SALT COD)

We use desalinated rehydrated salt cod fillets. These are available from Spanish grocers. If you can't find desalinated rehydrated salt cod, buy dried salt cod fillets and desalinate and rehydrate them yourself. You'll need to do this two days before you plan to use them. Brush off any visible salt crystals from the cod, place skin-side up in a large stainless steel bowl and cover with cold water. Refrigerate for 48 hours, changing the water every 12 hours. Remove the skin and bones and discard. Cover the flesh with plastic wrap and refrigerate until ready to use — treat the cod as you would fresh fish and use within a day or two. About 250 g (9 oz) salt cod, when rehydrated, will yield about 400 g (14 oz). You can buy dried salt cod fillets from Italian and Spanish grocers, delicatessens and gourmet food stores.

BAKER'S FLOUR

This is flour that has a higher protein content, making it suitable for baking bread. It is available in select supermarkets, gourmet food stores and bakeries.

BAY LEAVES

Use fresh bay leaves, available from greengrocers. If you have space, plant a tree.

BOMBA RICE

A type of short-grain rice grown in Spain. A whole culture of rice dishes (see pages 176–93) has evolved from this rice. Bomba takes about 18 minutes to cook. You can buy it from Spanish grocers and gourmet food stores.

BOQUERONES

These are anchovies that, instead of being salted, are preserved with vinegar. Soft white and delicious, they are perfect on a toothpick with an olive or give a sharp, hot tang to a salad of summer vegetables. I love that boquerón is southern Spanish slang for bogan, chav or red neck.

CHEESE

Spanish cheeses have a particular tang that is unmistakably, well, Spanish. Good cheese shops, delicatessens and some good small supermarkets will help you source the cheeses mentioned in this book.

CHORIZO

A pork sausage spiced with pimentón (paprika). The dried version is eaten as a snack like salami. The fresh version is used extensively in Spanish cooking. Beware, there are a lot of inferior sausages labelled as chorizo sold in butchers and supermarkets, so always make the effort to buy them from a good delicatessen.

CONSERVAS

If the Spanish catch or grow something good, they put it in cans or jars to preserve it and call them conservas. These include anchovies, small sardines, peaches, pickled garlic, guindillas and pimientos de piquillo, which we have used in this book.

CREAM CANISTERS

Cream canisters and soda bulbs are available from specialist kitchenware stores. It's important to buy a canister that can hold hot as well as cold liquids.

DIGITAL SCALES

Baking is a precise affair. A few grams out, especially with ingredients such as yeast, and the final outcome can be affected. We always use digital scales for accuracy.

DRINKING CHOCOLATE

Spanish drinking chocolate comes in a block, which you melt in hot milk. It contains a little flour to thicken hot chocolate. You can buy it from Spanish grocers and gourmet food stores.

EGGS

The recipes in this book use 55 g (2 oz) eggs. We only use organic, free-range eggs because they make food taste like traditional Spanish dishes. All recipes, unless stated otherwise, require eggs to be at room temperature.

EXTRA VIRGIN OLIVE OIL

As they say, oils ain't oils. For deep-frying we use sunflower oil, just as they do in the south of Spain. When we're starting off a dish such as braising or making a sofrito, we use a good extra virgin olive oil. We save the best till last, dressing dishes just before they head to the table with really good quality extra virgin olive such as the Spanish variety arbequina for fish dishes or manzanilla for heavier dishes that need a little kick.

FOOD DEHYDRATOR

This is a device that circulates slightly heated air over a series of mesh trays. Over several hours the moisture in food is evaporated and the food, such as fruits, dehydrate and are therefore preserved to some extent. They can be purchased from some health food stores, appliance centres and online.

GUINDILLAS

These are thin spicy sweet green peppers from the Basque country packed in white wine vinegar. They are available from Spanish grocers and gourmet food stores.

JAMÓN

This is air-dried and aged Spanish ham. There are several grades of jamón. Jamón serrano is from white pigs and is the most affordable. Next is jamón Ibérico, made from native black pigs. Jamón Iberico de bellota is the Rolls-Royce of Spanish ham. It is made from black pigs fed on acorns. Make sure you buy it freshly sliced from butchers and delicatessens to ensure the best quality and taste.

MEAT GLUE

This is a naturally occurring enzyme that is sprinkled on meat and seafood to break down some of the protein, which then allows it to bond again and you can stick two surfaces together. It's available from specialty stores and online.

MORCILLA

A Spanish blood sausage spiced with cinnamon. Black pudding can be substituted.

NUTS

Almonds, hazelnuts and pine nuts are used extensively in Spanish food. Nuts are packed with oil that goes rancid quickly, so buy them from shops where there is a high turnover of product. We buy ours from Middle Eastern grocers.

PARSLEY

Use flat-leaf (Italian) parsley unless stated otherwise.

PEROL PAN

A pan with high sides and a rounded base for making traditional wet rice dishes. A large high-sided saucepan will do the job perfectly well, too.

PICKLED GARLIC

This is a Spanish delicacy. It is a delicious little treat, typically served in tapas bars to punctuate a dish with its sharp cut and crunch. It is sold in jars, available from Spanish grocers and gourmet food stores.

PIMENTÓN

Spanish paprika comes in different varieties, made from dried spicy, sweet and bittersweet peppers. The pimentón from La Vera, smoked over oak, is particularly delicious. We typically use pimentón dulce ahumado (smoked sweet Spanish paprika) in this book.

PIMIENTOS DE PIQUILLO (PIQUILLO PEPPERS)

Spanish roasted red peppers packed in jars or tins. They are available from delicatessens and gourmet food stores.

PRESSURE COOKER

Water boils at 100 degrees at sea level. Increase the air pressure and it boils at a higher temperature. Put food in a pressure cooker and it cooks at a higher temperature, so the food cooks in less time. It is particularly good for cooking chickpeas and tough meats.

PULSES

These are Spanish staples. Chickpeas (garbanzos) and dried beans are the traditional protein of the poor. We use quality pulses from stores with a high turnover, particulary Middle Eastern and Indian grocers.

QUESO DE MAHÓN

Mahón is the capital of the rocky island of Menorca, off the coast of Spain. This is also the name given to all cow's milk cheeses produced here, ranging from young to very mature cheeses that are often rubbed with olive oil and paprika. After ripening on wooden shelves for 2–3 months, the cheese develops a slightly sweet aroma and mild buttery flavour that improves with age.

QUESO DE MANCHEGO

Manchego is a sheep's milk cheese from the La Mancha area of Spain. It's made into medium-sized rounds. Some Manchego is aged for 6 months, some for several years. During this period, cracking occurs along the curds and small flavoursome crystals form. It is a sweet cheese, sharp and tangy with a hint of earth.

QUESO DE VALDEÓN

A rich, creamy, full-flavoured cow's and goat's milk blue cheese made in caves in the north of Spain and traditionally wrapped in sycamore leaves, which were originally used to hold the fragile cheese together as it was transported down the mountains.

RENNET

This is an enzyme made from calf stomach used in cheesemaking to set milk into curds. Once available as junket tablets in supermarkets, it is now hard to come by, but you can buy it online from www.simplyjunket or www.cheeselinks.com.au.

SAFFRON

A spice made from the stamens of a crocus flower. By weight, saffron is more valuable than gold. Spanish saffron is best. Buy a very small box and use it judiciously.

SALT

We use different salts for different purposes. Black sea salt from Cyprus and pink Himalayan salt for looks and taste, sea salt for depth of flavour, flakes for crunch, fine salt for curing and rock salt for presenting oysters. Look out for these different types of salt at select supermarkets, delicatessens and gourmet food stores. Sometimes we use good old cooking salt too.

SARDINILLAS

These small Spanish sardines are available from Spanish grocers and gourmet food stores.

SHERRY

By law, sherry can only come from a little patch of Spain around a town called Jerez de la Frontera. We use fino (dry), oloroso (darker, slightly sweeter) and Pedro Ximénez (sweet). I'm a big fan of manzanilla, which is a fino sherry made in the seaside town of Sanlúcar de Barrameda.

THERMOMETER

The temperatures many of the dishes in this book are cooked at, especially those cooked using sous vide, are precise. An accurate thermometer is essential, we recommend a digital thermometer with a probe.

TOCINO

Tocino is pig back fat. Available from good butchers. You will need to order it in advance.

TOMATOES

Quite a few recipes in this book call for tomatoes to be peeled and seeded. To peel a tomato, score a cross at the base. Place in a heatproof bowl and cover with boiling water. Leave for about 30 seconds (less time for smaller tomatoes such as cherry tomatoes), then drain, refresh in cold water and peel the skin off away from the cross. To remove the seeds, cut the tomato in half and scoop out the seeds. Use the tomato flesh as directed.

VINEGAR

Good vinegar is essential to a good dish. We use chardonnay vinegar and Spanish sherry vinegar, available from gourmet food stores.

YEAST

We always use fresh yeast at MoVida. You can purchase this from bakeries, health food stores and Italian grocers. If it's not available, substitute half the amount of active dried yeast and use according to the manufacturer's instructions.

INDEX/INDICE

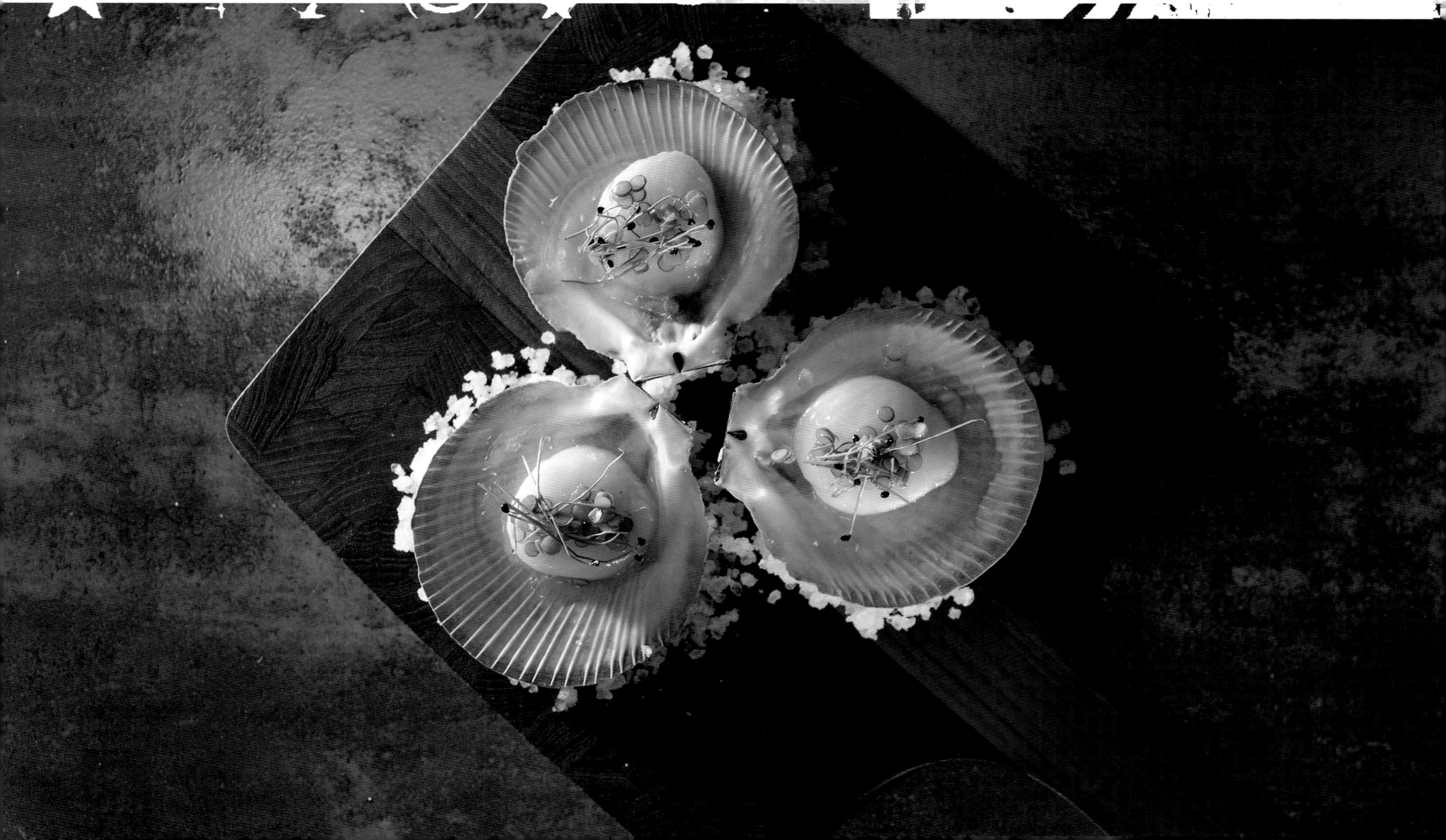

Published in 2011 by Murdoch Books Pty Limited

Murdoch Books Australia
Pier 8/9
23 Hickson Road
Millers Point NSW 2000
Phone: +61 (0) 2 8220 2000
Fax: +61 (0) 2 8220 2558
www.murdochbooks.com.au
info@murdochbooks.com.au

For Corporate Orders & Custom Publishing
contact Noel Hammond, National Business
Development Manager

Murdoch Books UK Limited
Erico House, 6th Floor
93–99 Upper Richmond Road
Putney, London SW15 2TG
Phone: +44 (0) 20 8785 5995
Fax: +44 (0) 20 8785 5985
www.murdochbooks.co.uk
info@murdochbooks.co.uk

Publisher: Kylie Walker
Art Direction/Designer: Reuben Crossman
Photographer: Alan Benson
Merchandising/Propping: Neil Hargreaves
Project Editor: Gabriella Sterio
Editor: Belinda So
Production: Renee Melbourne

National Library of Australia Cataloguing-in-
Publication Data

Author: Camorra, Frank; Cornish, Richard.
Title: Movida Cocina: Spanish Flavours
         From Five Kitchens / Frank Camorra
         and Richard Cornish.
ISBN: 978-1-74196-899-6 (hbk.)
Notes: Includes index.
Subjects: Cooking, Spanish.
Dewey Number: 641.5946

A catalogue record for this book is available
from the British Library.

PRINTED in 2011 by 1010 International
Printing Ltd, China.

IMPORTANT: Those who might be at risk from
the effects of salmonella poisoning (the elderly,
pregnant women, young children and those
suffering from immune deficiency diseases)
should consult their doctor with any concerns
about eating raw eggs.

OVEN GUIDE: You may find cooking times vary
depending on the oven you are using. For fan-
forced ovens, as a general rule, set the oven
temperature to 20°C (35°F) lower than indicated
in the recipe.